Kitchen Items

PATC
FOR   N

We will use friangle, square patchwork for hand made kitchen items
From now on favorite hobbies will be cooking and patchwork.

WALL HANGING WITH POCKE

Instructions on page 2

Handy wall hanging for the kitchen
Great for recipes and memos!

[ACTUAL SIZE]
You'll find cute patchwork fabrics

Heart applique

Kitchen
WALL HANGING WITH POCKET
page 1

Materials

Pink cotton (including patchwork fabric) 70cm×55cm (27 9/16″×21 11/16″)

Pink stripe cotton (including patchwork fabric) 90cm×75cm(35 7/16″×29 1/2″)

Patchwork, Appliqué cottons (Refer to the picture)

Offwhite cotton fabric
Batting 95cm×90cm(37 7/16″×35 7/16″)
Quilt thread...Offwhite

Finished size... Refer to illustration

☆Seam allowance is indicated in( )
(seam is 1cm(3/8″))

Basic fabric

Outer fabric...Pink } 1 each
Lining...Stripe

Batting [Cut 46cm×56cm (18 1/8″×22″) 2 pieces]

Outer=50cm(19 11/16″)
Lining=50cm (19 11/16″)

Outer fabric=40cm(15 3/4″)
Lining=44cm(17 5/16″)

(seam is 1cm(3/8″))

Pocket

Lining...Stripe
Batting [Cut 42cm ×15cm(16 1/2″6″)] } 3 each

40cm(15 3/4″)

−14cm(5 1/2″)

Border strip
Pink   (seam is 1cm (3/8″))
2cm(3/4″)

Offwhite 4 pieces
(seam is 1cm (3/8″))

Ⓐ=50cm (19 11/16″)
Ⓑ=40cm (15 1/2″)
2 each

Ⓒ=2cm(3/8″)

Stick case
Pink 3 pieces
10cm(4″)
(seam is 1cm (3/8″))
←7cm→
(2 3/4″)

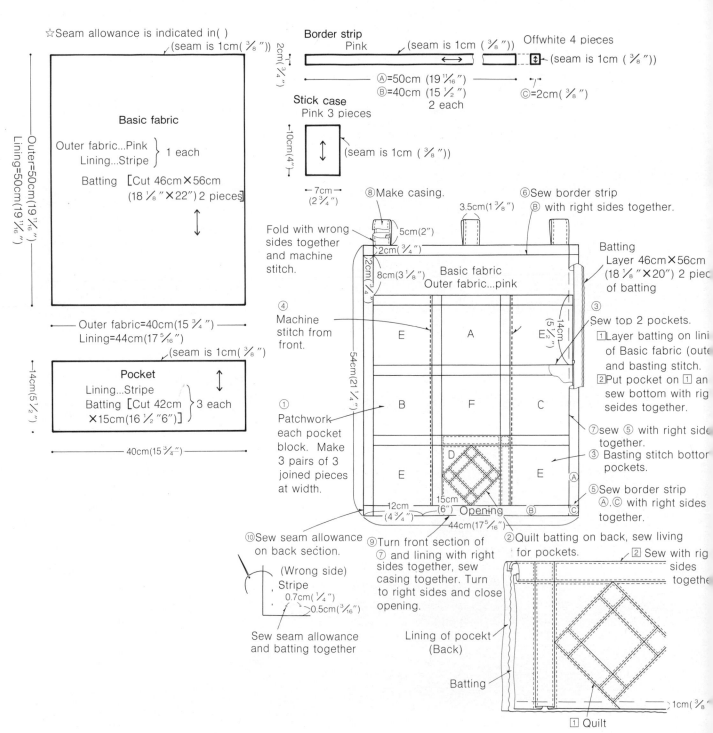

⑧Make casing.

Fold with wrong sides together and machine stitch.

5cm(2″)
2cm(3/4″)
2cm(3/4″)
8cm(3 1/8″)

④ Machine stitch from front.

① Patchwork each pocket block. Make 3 pairs of 3 joined pieces at width.

⑥Sew border strip Ⓑ with right sides together.

3.5cm(1 3/8″)

Batting
Layer 46cm×56cm (18 1/8″×20″) 2 piec of batting

Basic fabric
Outer fabric...pink

E   A
B   F   C
E   D   E

54cm(21 1/4″)
14cm(5 1/2″)

12cm(4 3/4″)
15cm(6″)
Opening
44cm(17 5/16″)

③ Sew top 2 pockets.
① Layer batting on lini of Basic fabric (oute and basting stitch.
② Put pocket on ① an sew bottom with rig seides together.

⑦sew ⑤ with right side together.
③ Basting stitch bottor pockets.

⑤Sew border strip Ⓐ.Ⓒ with right sides together.

⑩Sew seam allowance on back section.

(Wrong side)
Stripe
0.7cm(1/4″)
0.5cm(3/16″)

Sew seam allowance and batting together

⑨Turn front section of ⑦ and lining with right sides together, sew casing together. Turn to right sides and close opening.

②Quilt batting on back, sew living for pockets.

② Sew with rig sides togethe

Lining of pocekt (Back)

Batting

Lining of pocket (Back)

① Quilt

1cm(3/8)

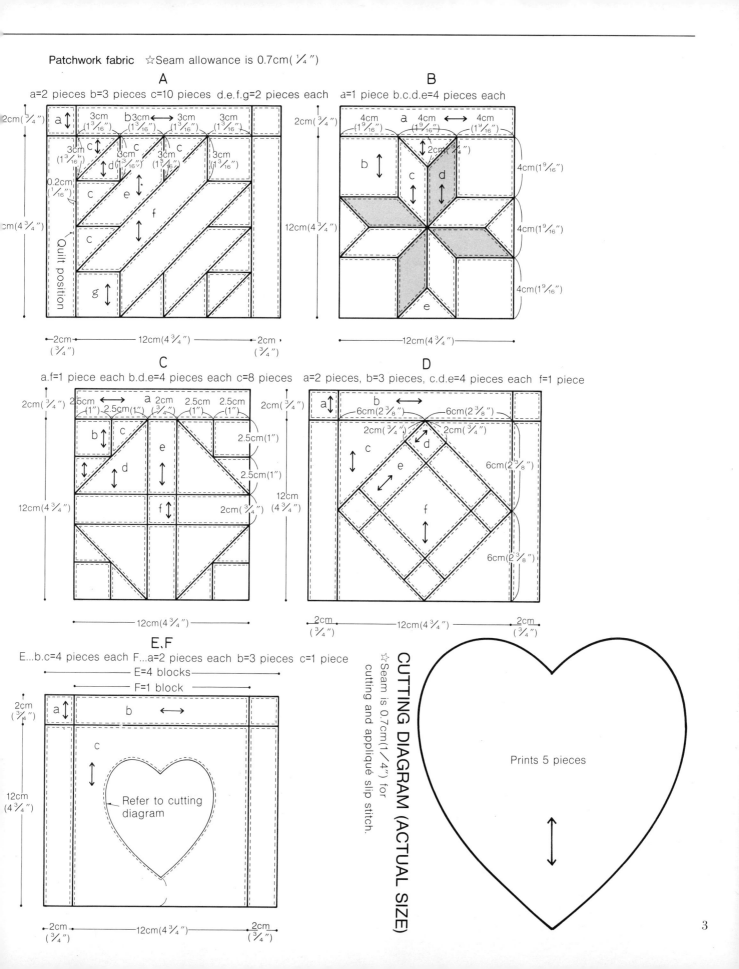

Patchwork fabric ☆Seam allowance is 0.7cm(¼")

A

a=2 pieces b=3 pieces c=10 pieces d.e.f.g=2 pieces each

B

a=1 piece b.c.d.e=4 pieces each

C

a.f=1 piece each b.d.e=4 pieces each c=8 pieces

D

a=2 pieces, b=3 pieces, c.d.e=4 pieces each f=1 piece

E.F

E...b.c=4 pieces each F...a=2 pieces each b=3 pieces c=1 piece

E=4 blocks

F=1 block

Refer to cutting diagram

CUTTING DIAGRAM (ACTUAL SIZE)

☆Seam is 0.7cm(1/4") for cutting and appliqué slip stitch.

Prints 5 pieces

3

Kitchen
POT HOLDER (MITTEN SHAPE, ROUND SHAPE) AND TOASTER COVER

Instruction
Pot holder on page 6
Toaster cover on page 27

Toaster cover is square shape, simple patchwork. Helps protect against dust and kitchen spills.

Patchwork is only on the right side.
That's easy to make.

Enjoy something handmade.

[ACTUAL SIZE]
Backstitch embroidery is the point!

Kitchen
POT HPLDER
page 4.5

(MITTEN AHSPE)
Materials
Offwhite quilt fabric 44cm×28cm (17 5/16"11")
White towel fabric 44cm×28cm (17 5/16"11")
Cotton fabric for patchwork (Refer to picture)

Blue bias strip 40cm(15 ¾")
1.6cm(⅝") wide
Quilt thread...Offwhite
Finished size...25.2cm(9 15/16") depth

Cutting Diagram (actual size)
☆Seam allowance is indicated in( )

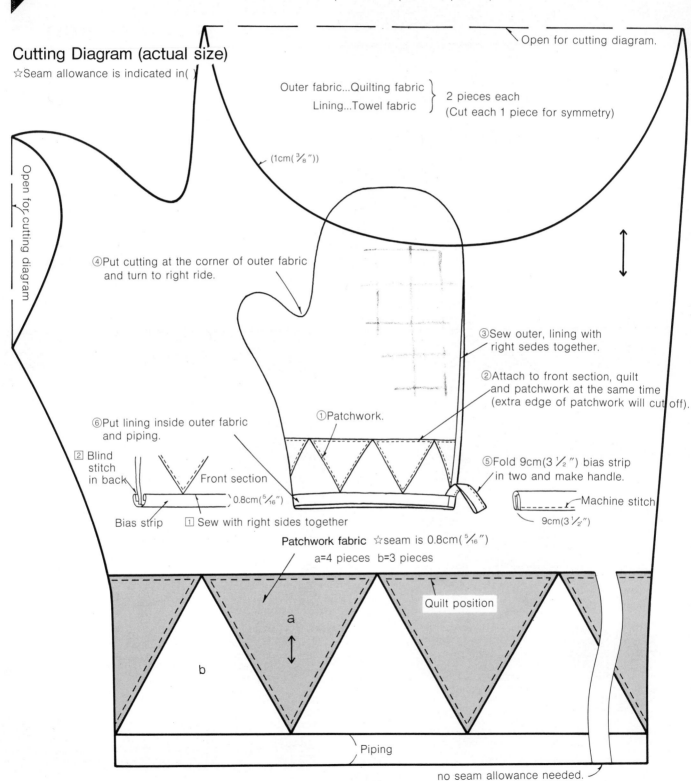

Open for cutting diagram.

Outer fabric...Quilting fabric
Lining...Towel fabric
} 2 pieces each
(Cut each 1 piece for symmetry)

(1cm(⅜"))

Open for cutting diagram

④Put cutting at the corner of outer fabric and turn to right ride.

③Sew outer, lining with right sedes together.

②Attach to front section, quilt and patchwork at the same time (extra edge of patchwork will cut off).

⑥Put lining inside outer fabric and piping.

①Patchwork.

② Blind stitch in back

Front section

Bias strip

0.8cm(5/16")

① Sew with right sides together

⑤Fold 9cm(3 ½") bias strip in two and make handle.

Machine stitch

9cm(3 ½")

Patchwork fabric ☆seam is 0.8cm(5/16")
a=4 pieces b=3 pieces

Quilt position

a

b

Piping

no seam allowance needed.

⟨ROUND SHAPE⟩

Materials (for I)

Offwhite shirting fabric
left side...40cm×20cm(15 ¾″×7 ⅞″)
right side...40cm×35cm(15 ¾″×17 ¾″)

Patchwork fabric (Refer to picture)
Quilt batting 20cm(7 ⅞″) square.
Green bias strip 80cm(31 ½″) 1.6cm(⅝″) wide
#25 embroidery floss Right side...Green
Quilt thread...Green. Offwhite

Finished size...20cm(7 ⅞″) diameter

☆Seam allowance is indicated in ( )
Outer fabric, Lining...Offwhite
Batting } 1 each

[Right]

20cm(7 ⅞″)
(no seam allowance is needed.)

④Fold 12cm(4 ¾″) bias strip in two and make handle.
—12cm(4 ¾″)—
Machine stitch

①Patchwork embroider center for right side.
②Put it on outer fabric and quilt. Ⓐ
(Quilt thread and fabric is same color)
③Layer batting on ② and quilt. Ⓑ

0.8cm(⁵⁄₁₆″)
Piping

⑤Layer lining on ③, put handle in and piping around edge.
(Wrong side)
0.8cm(⁵⁄₁₆″)
2 Blind stitch on back.
1 Sew with right sides together.

EMBROIDERY DIAGRAM (ACTUAL SIZE)
3 strands

Back stitch

Patchwork fabric   ☆Seam is 0.7cm(¼″)

Left
a.b=2 pieces each

Ⓐ

Ⓑ   Quilt position

—6cm(2 ⅜″)—6cm(2 ⅜″)—

Right
a.b=2 pieces each c=1 piece

6cm(2 ⅜″)
6cm(2 ⅜″)

Ⓐ
Ⓑ

—6cm(2 ⅜″)—6cm(2 ⅜″)—

Straight stitch

Back stitch

Running stitch

Satin stitch

Lazydaisy stitch

French knot stitch

Chain stitch

Cross stitch

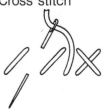

Kitchen

NAPKIN

Instructions on page 10

A cloth with many uses. Use it to cover a basket or as a pot holder.

Lemon star pattern patchwork

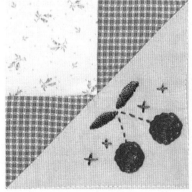

Embroider pink fabric at edge and appliqué

DISH CASE
AND MAT

Instructions on page 11

Use this to store and protect your favorite china.

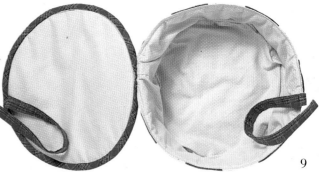

Embroidery on mat Lid of dish case. Embroidery in one line.

When you open the lid, it's lined with cute polka doats.

9

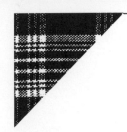

Kitchen NAPKIN

page8

<SQUARE PATCH NAPKIN>

Materials

[] is blue color, common unless indicated otherwise.

Pink [blue] flower pattern cotton Ⓐ (including patchwork cloth) 89cm×42cm(35″×16 ½″)

Pink [blue] flower pattern cotton Ⓑ 32cm(12 $^{9}/_{16}$″)square

Pink [blue] check cotton 30cm(11 $^{13}/_{16}$″) square

Pink [blue] plain cloth 14cm(5 ½″) square

#25 embroidery floss...Olive green, Coral red, [Deep green, Blue]

Finished size...40cm(15 ¾″) square

☆Seam allowance is indicated in( )

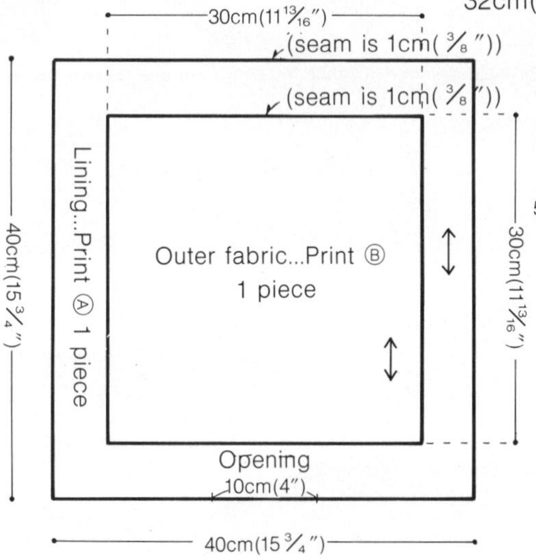

30cm(11 $^{13}/_{16}$″)
(seam is 1cm(⅜″))
(seam is 1cm(⅜″))
Lining...Print Ⓐ 1 piece
Outer fabric...Print Ⓑ
1 piece
40cm(15 ¾″)
30cm(11 $^{13}/_{16}$″)
Opening
10cm(4″)
40cm(15 ¾″)

Patchwork fabric (Refer to picture)
☆seam is 0.8cm($^{5}/_{16}$″)
a.b...14 pieces each

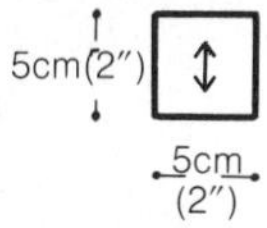

5cm(2″)
5cm
(2″)

Appliqué fabric
☆fold is 0.8cm($^{5}/_{16}$″)
Plain 2 pieces

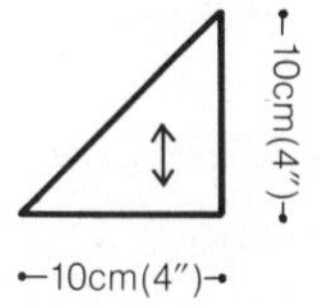

10cm(4″)
10cm(4″)

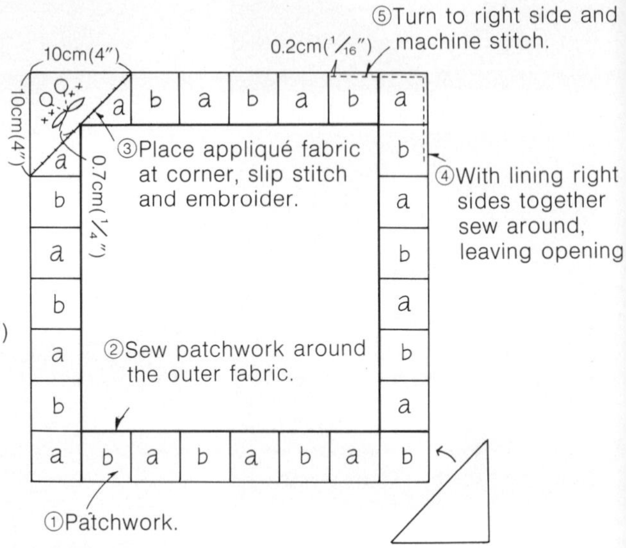

⑤Turn to right side and machine stitch.
0.2cm($^{1}/_{16}$″)
10cm(4″)
10cm(4″)
0.7cm(¼″)
③Place appliqué fabric at corner, slip stitch and embroider.
④With lining right sides together sew around, leaving opening
②Sew patchwork around the outer fabric.
①Patchwork.

EMBROIDERY DIAGRAM IS ON PAGE 15.

<LEMON STAR NAPKIN>

Materials

[] is blue color, common unless indicated other wise.

Red [Blue] Plain fabric (including patchwork fabric) 55cm×25cm(21 ⅝″×10″)

Red [Blue] Cotton print... 42cm(16 ½″) square

Offwhite cotton fabric 48cm×22cm (18(⅞″×8 $^{11}/_{16}$″)

Patchwork fabric (Refer to picture)

#25 embroidery floss...Coral red [Blue]

Quilt thread...Offwihte

Finished size...40cm(15 ¾″) square

☆Seam allowance is indicated in ( )

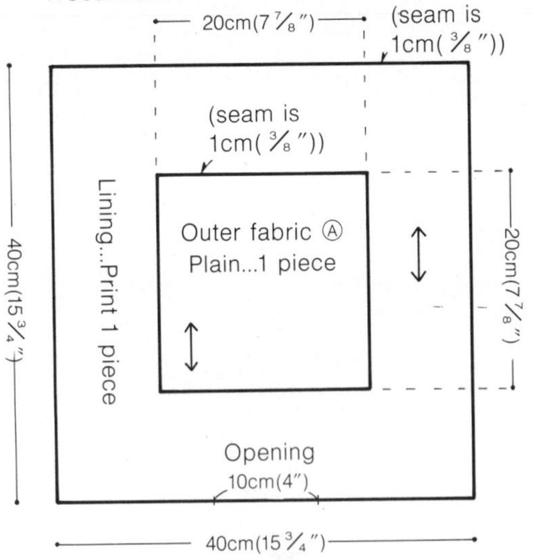

20cm(7 ⅞″)
(seam is 1cm(⅜″))
(seam is 1cm(⅜″))
Lining...Print 1 piece
Outer fabric Ⓐ
Plain...1 piece
40cm(15 ¾″)
20cm(7 ⅞″)
Opening
10cm(4″)
40cm(15 ¾″)

Patchwork fabric ☆Seam is 0.8cm($^{5}/_{16}$″)
a.b.c.d=8 pieces each e.f=16 pieces each

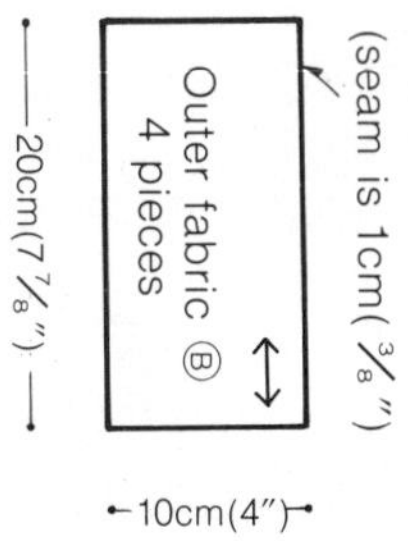

20cm(7 ⅞″)
Outer fabric Ⓑ
4 pieces
(seam is 1cm(⅜″)
10cm(4″)

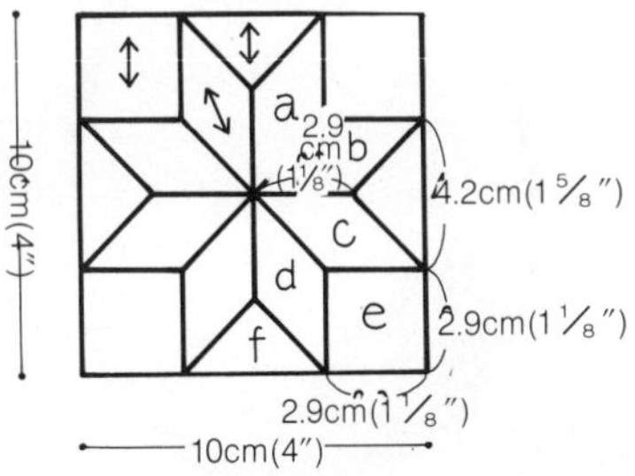

10cm(4″)
a
b
c
d
e
f
2.9cm(1⅛″)
4.2cm(1⅝″)
2.9cm(1⅛″)
2.9cm(1⅛″)
10cm(4″)

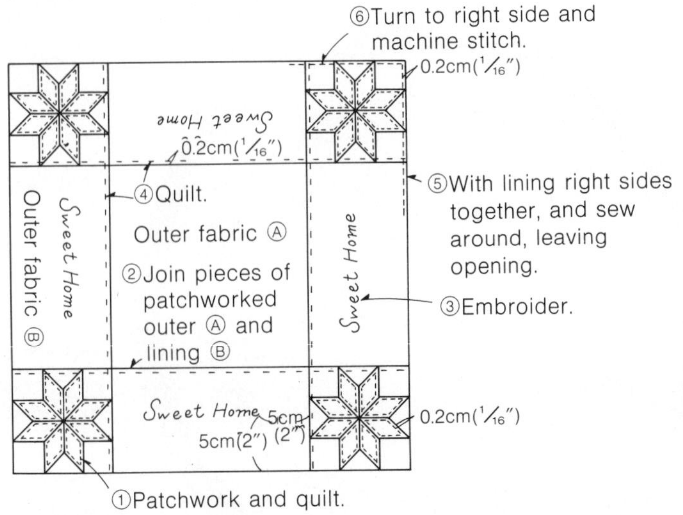

⑥Turn to right side and machine stitch.
0.2cm($^{1}/_{16}$″)
Sweet Home
0.2cm($^{1}/_{16}$″)
④Quilt.
Outer fabric Ⓑ
Sweet Home
Outer fabric Ⓐ
②Join pieces of patchworked outer Ⓐ and lining Ⓑ
Sweet Home
⑤With lining right sides together, and sew around, leaving opening.
③Embroider.
Sweet Home
5cm(2″)
5cm(2″)
0.2cm($^{1}/_{16}$″)
①Patchwork and quilt.

EMBROIDERY DIAGRAM IS ON PAGE 15

Kitchen
DISH CASE AND MAT
page 9

Materials
Check suede cotton 90cm×105cm (35 7/16″×41 5/16″)
Offwhite suede cotton 90cm×25cm (35 7/16″×10″)
Pink polka dots cotton 72cm×36cm (28 5/16″×14 3/16″)

Batting 90cm×55cm(35 7/16″×21 11/16″)
#25 embroidery floss...Red
Quilt thread...Red
Finished size...Refer to illustration

☆Seam allowance is indicated in ( ) no seam is needed otherwise

Lid
23cm(9″)
Outer fabric...Offwhite
Lining...Polka dots
Batting   1 each

10cm(4″)
Opening (Only lining)
Bottom
22cm(8 11/16″)
(seam is 1cm(3/8″))

Dish Mat
20cm(7 7/8″)
Check...10 pieces
Batting...5 pieces
Outer fabric...Check
Lining...Polka dots
Batting   1 each

Strip
4cm(1 1/2″) Check 2 pieces
27cm(10 5/8″)

(seam is 1cm(3/8″))
Side section
Lining...Polka dots
Batting   1 each
10cm(4″)
70cm(27 1/2″)

Patchwork fabric ☆seam is 1cm(3/8″)
Check
Offwhite } 14 pieces each
5cm(2″)
5cm (2″)

Appliqué fabric
Offwhite 5 pieces
6cm(2 3/8″)
(seam is 1cm(3/8″))
6cm (2 3/8″)

Bias strip [] is dish mat
Lid...1 piece
Dish mat...5 pieces
4cm(1 1/2″) Check
74cm(29 1/8″)
(65cm(25 5/8″))

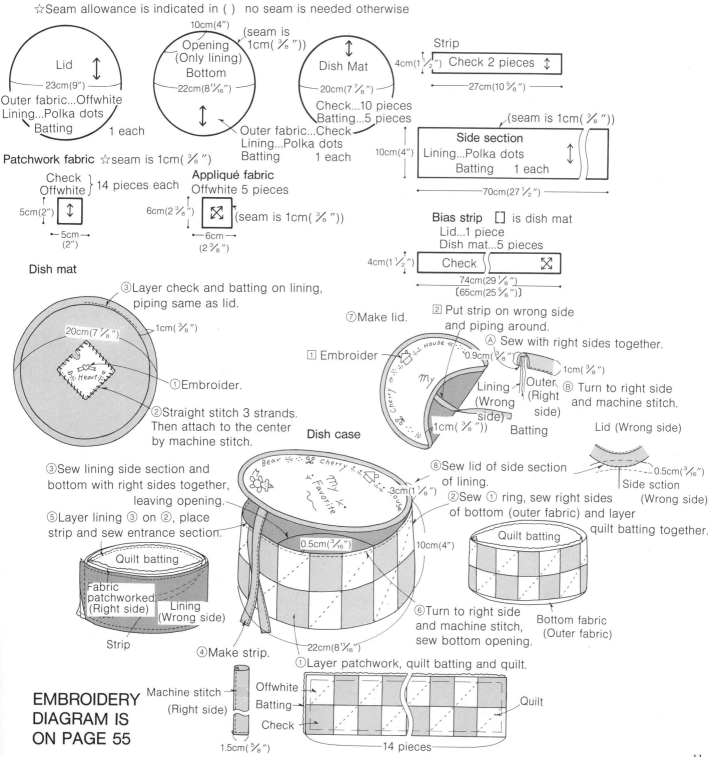

Dish mat

③Layer check and batting on lining, piping same as lid.
20cm(7 7/8″)
1cm(3/8″)
①Embroider.
②Straight stitch 3 strands. Then attach to the center by machine stitch.

⑦Make lid.
①Embroider
③Put strip on wrong side and piping around.
Ⓐ Sew with right sides together.
0.9cm(3/8″)
1cm(3/8″)
Lining (Wrong side)
Outer (Right side)
Ⓑ Turn to right side and machine stitch.
Batting
1cm(3/8″)
Lid (Wrong side)
0.5cm(3/16″)
Side sction (Wrong side)

Dish case

③Sew lining side section and bottom with right sides together, leaving opening.
⑤Layer lining ③ on ②, place strip and sew entrance section.
Quilt batting
Fabric patchworked (Right side)
Lining (Wrong side)
Strip
④Make strip.
22cm(8 11/16″)
0.5cm(3/16″)

⑧Sew lid of side section of lining.
3cm(1 1/8″)
②Sew ① ring, sew right sides of bottom (outer fabric) and layer quilt batting together.
Quilt batting
10cm(4″)
⑥Turn to right side and machine stitch, sew bottom opening.
Bottom fabric (Outer fabric)

①Layer patchwork, quilt batting and quilt.
Machine stitch (Right side)
Offwhite
Batting
Check
1.5cm(5/8″)
Offwhite
Batting
Check
Quilt
14 pieces

EMBROIDERY DIAGRAM IS ON PAGE 55

Kitchen
TABLE CLOTH, TEA COZY, NAPKIN

Instructions on page 14
Enjoy your coffee in the morning sunlight. with fresh blue coordinates.
Great for a holiday or any day.

→ Patchwork on napkin is same size as that of table cloth
[ACTUAL SIZE]

← A check pattern ribbon for handle is a cute addition.

[ACTUAL SIZE]
Star shape patchwork of table cloth

13

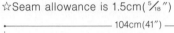

Kitchen
TABLECLOTH AND TEA COZY + NAPKIN
page 12.13

<TABLE CLOTH>
Materials

Light check cotton 110cm×260cm(43 5/16″×102 3/8″)

White cotton 40cm(15 3/4″) square

Blue cotton 35cm(13 3/4″) square

Dark check cotton 25cm(10″) square

Finished size...120cm(47 1/4″) square

☆Seam allowance is 1.5cm(5/8″)

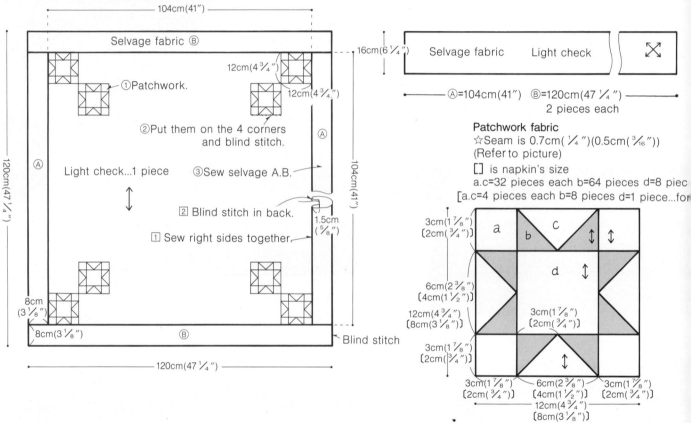

104cm(41″)

Selvage fabric Ⓑ

12cm(4 3/4″)

①Patchwork.

12cm(4 3/4″)

②Put them on the 4 corners and blind stitch.

Light check...1 piece

③Sew selvage A.B.

Ⓐ

120cm(47 1/4″)

104cm(41″)

Ⓐ

② Blind stitch in back.

① Sew right sides together.

1.5cm(5/8″)

8cm(3 1/8″)

8cm(3 1/8″)

Ⓑ

120cm(47 1/4″)

Blind stitch

16cm(6 1/4″)

Selvage fabric   Light check

Ⓐ=104cm(41″) Ⓑ=120cm(47 1/4″)
2 pieces each

Patchwork fabric

☆Seam is 0.7cm(1/4″)(0.5cm(3/16″))
(Refer to picture)

[] is napkin's size
a.c=32 pieces each b=64 pieces d=8 piec
[a.c=4 pieces each b=8 pieces d=1 piece...fo

3cm(1 7/8″) [2cm(3/4″)]

a   b   c

6cm(2 3/8″) [4cm(1 1/2″)]

d

12cm(4 3/4″) [8cm(3 1/8″)]

3cm(1 7/8″) [2cm(3/4″)]

3cm(1 7/8″) [2cm(3/4″)]

3cm(1 7/8″) [2cm(3/4″)]

6cm(2 3/8″) [4cm(1 1/2″)]

3cm(1 7/8″) [2cm(3/4″)]

12cm(4 3/4″) [8cm(3 1/8″)]

<NAPKIN>

Materials(for 1)

White cotton 48cm(18 7/8″)square

Blue, Light, Dark check cotton, a little

Finished size...44cm(17 5/16″) square

☆Seam is 2cm(3/4″)

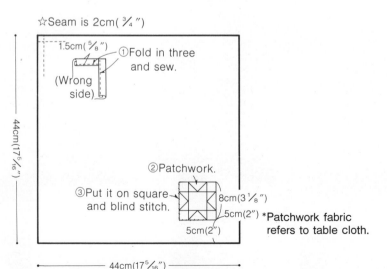

1.5cm(5/8″)

①Fold in three and sew.

(Wrong side)

44cm(17 5/16″)

②Patchwork.

③Put it on square and blind stitch.

8cm(3 1/8″)

5cm(2″)

5cm(2″)

*Patchwork fabric refers to table cloth.

44cm(17 5/16″)

‹TEA COZY›

Materials
Blue cotton 90cm×60cm
(35 $\frac{7}{16}$ "×23 $\frac{5}{8}$ ")
Check cotton 20cm(7 $\frac{7}{8}$ ") square
White cotton 20cm(7 $\frac{7}{8}$ ") square
Batting 55cm×45cm
(21 $\frac{11}{16}$ "×17 $\frac{11}{16}$ ")
Synthetic cotton
Finished size...Refer to illustration

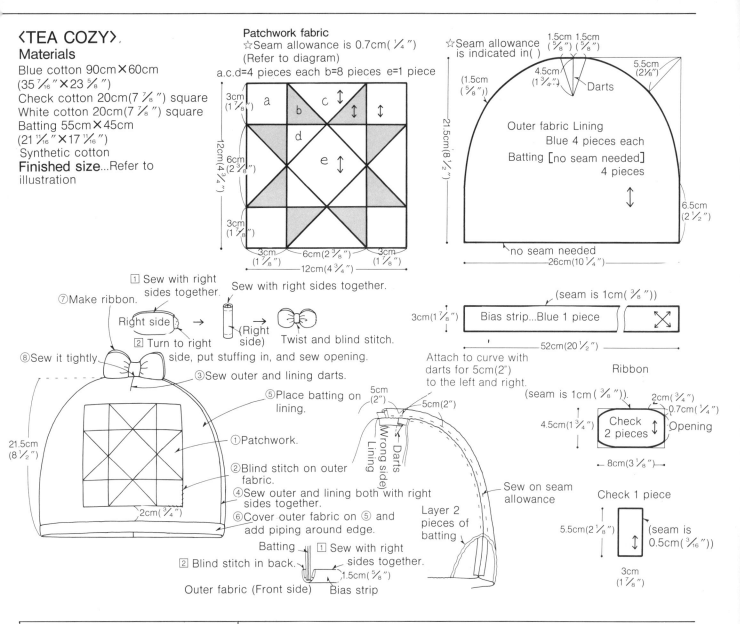

Patchwork fabric
☆Seam allowance is 0.7cm($\frac{1}{4}$ ")
(Refer to diagram)
a.c.d=4 pieces each b=8 pieces e=1 piece

3cm ($1\frac{7}{8}$ ") a b c
6cm ($2\frac{3}{8}$ ") d
e
3cm ($1\frac{7}{8}$ ")
12cm (4 $\frac{3}{4}$ ")
3cm ($1\frac{7}{8}$ ") 6cm(2 $\frac{3}{8}$ ") 3cm ($1\frac{7}{8}$ ")
12cm(4 $\frac{3}{4}$ ")

☆Seam allowance is indicated in( )

1.5cm ($\frac{5}{8}$ ") 1.5cm ($\frac{5}{8}$ ")
4.5cm ($1\frac{3}{4}$ ") Darts
5.5cm ($2\frac{1}{8}$ ")
(1.5cm ($\frac{5}{8}$ "))
(1.5cm ($\frac{5}{8}$ "))
21.5cm(8 $\frac{1}{2}$ ")
Outer fabric Lining
Blue 4 pieces each
Batting [no seam needed]
4 pieces
6.5cm (2 $\frac{1}{2}$ ")
no seam needed
26cm(10 $\frac{1}{4}$ ")

⑦Make ribbon.
① Sew with right sides together.
Sew with right sides together.
Right side →
→ (Right side)
② Turn to right side, put stuffing in, and sew opening.
Twist and blind stitch.
⑧Sew it tightly.
③Sew outer and lining darts.
⑤Place batting on lining.
21.5cm (8 $\frac{1}{2}$ ")
①Patchwork.
②Blind stitch on outer fabric.
④Sew outer and lining both with right sides together.
⑥Cover outer fabric on ⑤ and add piping around edge.
2cm ($\frac{3}{4}$ ")
5cm (2")
5cm(2")
Darts
Wrong side
Lining
Batting
① Sew with right sides together.
② Blind stitch in back.
1.5cm ($\frac{5}{8}$ ")
Outer fabric (Front side)
Bias strip
Layer 2 pieces of batting
Sew on seam allowance

(seam is 1cm($\frac{3}{8}$ "))
3cm(1 $\frac{7}{8}$ ")
Bias strip...Blue 1 piece
52cm(20 $\frac{1}{2}$ ")
Attach to curve with darts for 5cm(2") to the left and right.
Ribbon
(seam is 1cm($\frac{3}{8}$ ")).
4.5cm(1 $\frac{3}{4}$ ")
Check 2 pieces
2cm ($\frac{3}{4}$ ")
0.7cm($\frac{1}{4}$ ")
Opening
8cm(3 $\frac{1}{8}$ ")
Check 1 piece
5.5cm(2 $\frac{1}{8}$ ")
(seam is 0.5cm($\frac{3}{16}$ "))
3cm (1 $\frac{7}{8}$ ")

CONTINED FROM PAGE 10

EMBROIDERY DIAGRAM (ACTUAL SIZE)

☆3 strands unless indicated otherwise.

Satin stitch
Olive green [Light green]
Cross stitch
Back stitch
Coral red (Blue) 4 strands

Sweet Home

Fill up chain stitch.
Running stitch
Coral red [Blue]

KICHEN MAT
Instructions on page 18

This kitchen mat will warm up a cold floor.
Heart shapes will make it even cozier.

SHELF LINING
Instruction on page 19

Shelf Lining help prevent scratches.
Let's make this attractive and useful to fit your shelf.

See the matching colors
of the embroidery and patchwork

Kitchen
KICHEN MAT
page 16

Materials

Check cotton (including patchwork, appliqué fabric) 90cm×85cm(35 $\frac{7}{16}$"×33 $\frac{7}{16}$")
Red cotton 90cm×55cm(35 $\frac{7}{16}$"×21 $\frac{11}{16}$")
Patchwork, Appliqué fabric (Refer to picture)
Batting 70cm×48cm(27 $\frac{9}{16}$"×18 $\frac{7}{8}$")
Quilt thread...Offwhite nonskid backing 68cm×46cm(27 $\frac{1}{4}$"×18 $\frac{1}{8}$")
Finished size...75cm×48cm(29 $\frac{1}{2}$"×18 $\frac{7}{8}$")
(including decoration's of edge)

APPLIQUE DIAGRAM (ACTUAL SIZE)

a～e...2 pieces each

☆Add 0.5cm($\frac{3}{16}$") seam allowance when you cut it and appliqué slip stitch.

☆Seam allowance is indicated in( )

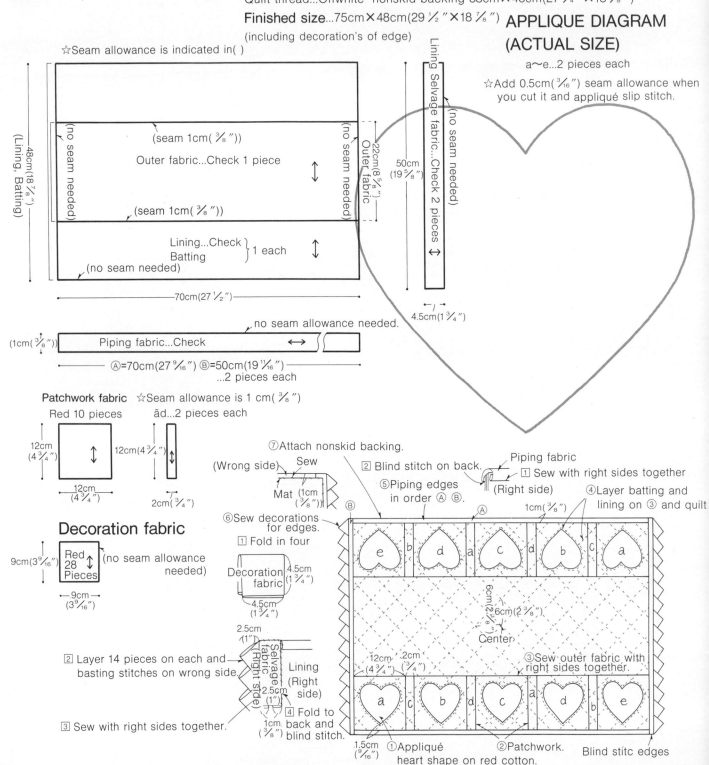

48cm(18 $\frac{7}{8}$") (Lining, Batting)

(no seam needed)
(seam 1cm($\frac{3}{8}$"))
Outer fabric...Check 1 piece
(seam 1cm($\frac{3}{8}$"))
(no seam needed)
Lining...Check } 1 each
Batting
(no seam needed)

70cm(27 $\frac{1}{2}$")

Lining Selvage fabric...Check 2 pieces
22cm(8 $\frac{5}{8}$") Outer fabric
50cm (19 $\frac{5}{8}$")
(no seam needed)
4.5cm(1 $\frac{3}{4}$")

(1cm($\frac{3}{8}$"))
Piping fabric...Check
no seam allowance needed.
Ⓐ=70cm(27 $\frac{9}{16}$") Ⓑ=50cm(19 $\frac{11}{16}$")
...2 pieces each

Patchwork fabric ☆Seam allowance is 1 cm($\frac{3}{8}$")

Red 10 pieces
12cm (4 $\frac{3}{4}$")
12cm (4 $\frac{3}{4}$")

ā̄d...2 pieces each
12cm(4 $\frac{3}{4}$")
2cm($\frac{3}{4}$")

Decoration fabric

9cm(3 $\frac{9}{16}$")
Red 28 Pieces
(no seam allowance needed)
9cm (3 $\frac{9}{16}$")

② Layer 14 pieces on each and basting stitches on wrong side.

③ Sew with right sides together.

⑦Attach nonskid backing.
(Wrong side) Sew
Mat (1cm ($\frac{3}{8}$"))
Ⓑ
② Blind stitch on back.
⑤Piping edges in order Ⓐ Ⓑ.
Piping fabric
① Sew with right sides together
(Right side)

⑥Sew decorations for edges.
① Fold in four
Decoration fabric 4.5cm (1 $\frac{3}{4}$")
4.5cm (1 $\frac{3}{4}$")

2.5cm (1")
Selvage fabric (Right side)
2.5cm (1")
Lining (Right side)
④ Fold to back and blind stitch.
1cm ($\frac{3}{8}$")

④Layer batting and lining on ③ and quilt
1cm($\frac{3}{8}$")

e b d a c d b c a

6cm(2 $\frac{3}{8}$")
6cm(2 $\frac{3}{8}$")
Center

12cm (4 $\frac{3}{4}$") 2cm ($\frac{3}{4}$")

③Sew outer fabric with right sides together.

a c b d c a d b e

1.5cm ($\frac{9}{16}$")
①Appliqué heart shape on red cotton.
②Patchwork.
Blind stitc edges

18

Kitchen
SHELF LINING
page 17

Materials (for 1)

Offwhite cotton 57cm×60cm(22 7/16″×23 5/8″)

Red check cotton 30cm×150cm(11 13/16″×6″)

Patchwork cotton (Refer to picture)

#25 embroidery floss...Red

Quilt thread...Offwhite

Finished size...55cm×32cm(21 11/16″×12 9/16″)

☆Seam allowance is indicated in ( )

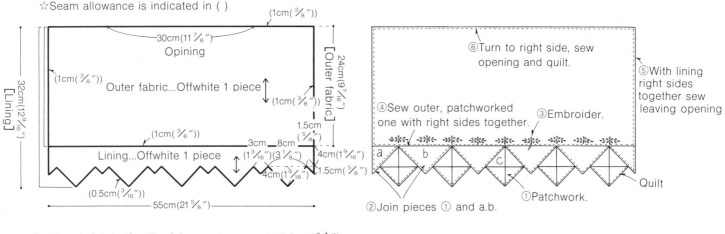

Patchwork fabric (for 1)   ☆Seam allowance is 0.5cm(3/16″)

a=Check 2 pieces   b=Check 4 pieces   c=20 pieces

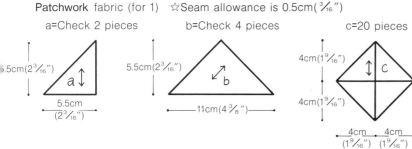

EMBROIDERY DIAGRAM (ACTUAL SIZE)
☆4 strands

Straight stitch

Lazydaisy stitch

French knot stitch

CONTINUED FROM PAGE 27

EMBROIDERY DIAGRAM (ACTUAL SIZE)
☆3 strands

Back stitch

French knot stitch

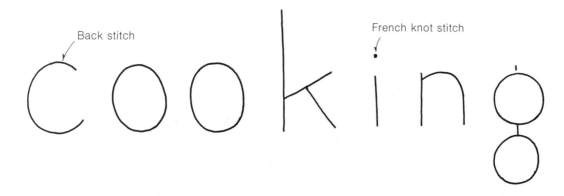

Kitchen
PLACE MAT,
TEA POT COVER,
HANDY BAG

Instructions

Place mat page 22

Tea pot cover page 23

Handy bag page 59

It's simple and fun to use cotton.
Enjoy using your favorite ideas,
colors, and shapes.

[ACTUAL SIZE]
Tea pot cover patchwork.
Size of tea pot cover will be the
height and longest width of the
pot.

[ACTUAL SIZE]
Pattern of the center
of place mat.

21

Kitchen
PLACE MAT
page 20.21

Materials (for 1)

Dark brown cotton 70cm×40cm(27 9/16″×15 3/4″)
Stripe cotton 18cm×41cm(7″×16 1/8″)
White cotton 30cm(11 13/16″) square
Check print cotton (Refer to picture)
Batting 42.1cm×30.7cm(16 9/16″×12″)
Quilt thread...Offwhite

☆Seam allowance is 1 cm(3/8 ″) **Finished size**...42.1cm×30.7cm(16 9/16 ″×12″)

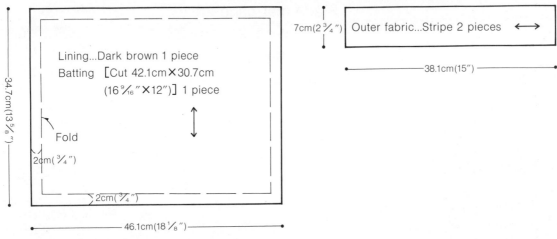

Lining...Dark brown 1 piece
Batting [Cut 42.1cm×30.7cm
(16 9/16″×12″)] 1 piece

Fold

2cm(3/4″)

2cm(3/4″)

34.7cm(13 5/8″)

46.1cm(18 1/8″)

7cm(2 3/4″)

Outer fabric...Stripe 2 pieces ←→

38.1cm(15″)

Patchwork fabric ☆Seam allowance is 0.7cm(1/4 ″)

a=3 pieces b.c=6 pieces each

3cm(1 3/16″) 3cm(1 3/16″)
3cm(1 3/16″) a b c
3cm(1 3/16″)
3cm(1 3/16″)
9cm(3 9/16″)
3cm(1 3/16″)
9cm(3 9/16″)

a~d=4 pieces each

3cm(1 3/16″)
a c d b
3cm(1 3/16″)
1.5cm(5/8″)
1.5cm(5/8″)
1.5cm(5/8″)
9cm(3 9/16″)

a.b=4 pieces each c=1 piece

4.5cm(1 3/4″) a b
c
2cm(3/4″)
4.5cm(1 3/4″)
9cm(3 9/16″)

4 pieces

0.1cm(1/16″)
1cm(3/8″) Quilt position
9cm(3 9/16″)

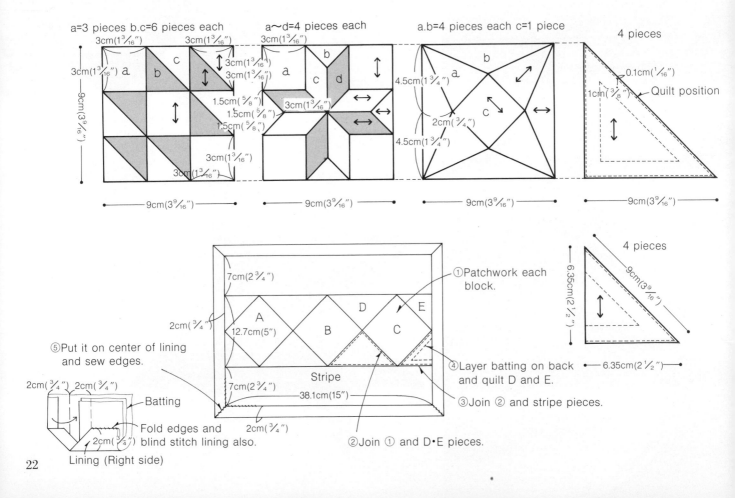

⑤Put it on center of lining
and sew edges.

2cm(3/4″) 2cm(3/4″)
Batting
Fold edges and blind stitch lining also.
2cm(3/4″)
Lining (Right side)

7cm(2 3/4″)

2cm(3/4″)

A
12.7cm(5″)

B

D

E

C

Stripe

7cm(2 3/4″)

38.1cm(15″)

2cm(3/4″)

①Patchwork each block.

④Layer batting on back
and quilt D and E.

③Join ② and stripe pieces.

②Join ① and D·E pieces.

4 pieces

6.35cm(2 1/2″)
9cm(3 9/16″)
6.35cm(2 1/2″)

Kitchen
TEA POT COVER
page 20.21

Materials

Check cotton...45cm×20cm(17¾″×7⅞″) (including patchwork fabric)

Dark brown cotton...35cm×20cm(13¾″×7⅞″)

Patchwork cotton (Refer to picture)

Batting 30cm×25cm(11¹³⁄₁₆″×10″)

0.5cm(³⁄₁₆″) wide green satin ribbon 60cm(23⅝″)

#25 embroidery floss...Dark brown

Quilt thread...Offfwhite

Finished size...Refer to illustration

☆Seam allowance is 1 cm (⅜ ″)

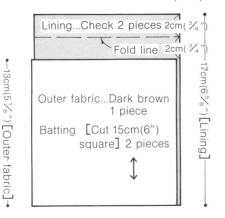

Lining...Check 2 pieces 2cm(¾″)

Fold line 2cm(¾″)

Outer fabric...Dark brown 1 piece

Batting [Cut 15cm(6″) square] 2 pieces

←13cm(5⅛″)[Outer fabric]→

17cm(6⅝″)[Lining]

13cm(5⅛″)

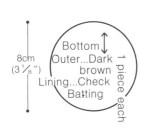

Bottom
Outer...Dark brown
Lining...Check
Batting

1 piece each

8cm(3⅛″)

Patchwork fabric ☆Seam allowance is 0.7cm(¼″)

a.b.c=4 pieces each f.g=2 pieces each d.e.h=1 piece each

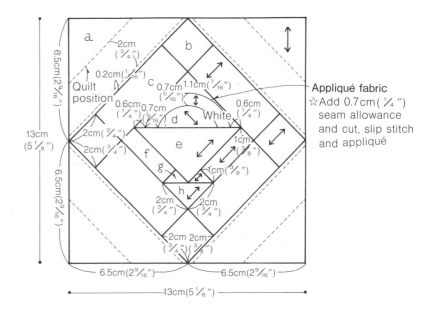

a
b
c
d
e
f
g
h

6.5cm(2⁹⁄₁₆″)

Quilt position

2cm(¾″)

0.2cm(¹⁄₁₆″)

0.7cm(⁵⁄₁₆″) 1.1cm(⁷⁄₁₆″)

0.6cm(¼″) 0.7cm(⁵⁄₁₆″)

0.6cm(¼″)

White

1cm(⅜″)

2cm(¾″)

2cm(¾″)

13cm(5⅛″)

6.5cm(2⁹⁄₁₆″)

1cm(⅜″)

2cm(¾″)

2cm(¾″)

2cm 2cm(¾″)(¾″)

6.5cm(2⁹⁄₁₆″)

6.5cm(2⁹⁄₁₆″)

13cm(5⅛″)

Appliqué fabric
☆Add 0.7cm(¼″) seam allowance and cut, slip stitch and appliqué

EMBROIDERY DIAGRAM (ACTUAL SIZE)

☆ 2 stands

Back stitch

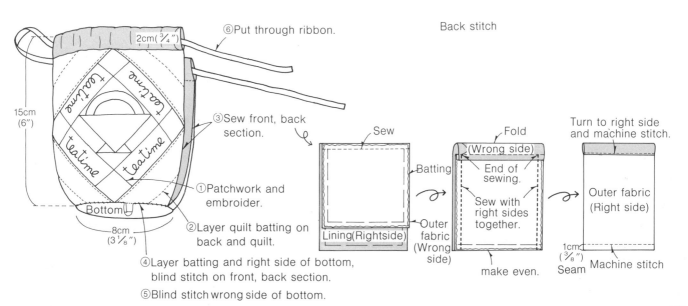

⑥Put through ribbon.

2cm(¾″)

15cm(6″)

③Sew front, back section.

①Patchwork and embroider.

②Layer quilt batting on back and quilt.

Bottom

8cm(3⅛″)

④Layer batting and right side of bottom, blind stitch on front, back section.

⑤Blind stitch wrong side of bottom.

Sew

Batting

Outer fabric (Wrong side)

Lining(Rightside)

Fold

(Wrong side)

End of sewing.

Sew with right sides together.

make even.

Turn to right side and machine stitch.

Outer fabric (Right side)

1cm(⅜″) Seam

Machine stitch

Kitchen
TABLE CENTER AND COASTERS

Instructions on page 26

The bright of these table center and coasters will reflect your warm hospitality.

"Cactus" coaster uses the same pattern as table center.

HEART-SHAPED BAG

Instructionsd on page 27

Very hand for keeping recipes or receipts.

Enjoy using it in the kitchen.

Back side of heart shape, heart shape all around.

Kitchen
TABLE CENTER & COASTERS
page 24

⟨TABLE CENTER⟩
Materials

Green print cotton...88.5cm×23cm (34 ⅞″×9″) (including appliqué fabric)
Light olive green cotton 53cm×27.5cm (20 ⅞″×10 ¹³⁄₁₆″)
Dark yellow print cotton 35cm(13 ¾″) square
Light gray print cotton 40cm×30cm (15 ¾″×11 ¹³⁄₁₆″)
Dark yellow broadcloth 25cm(10″) square
Cream color broadcloth 20cm(7 ⅞″) square
Quilt batting 59cm×33.5cm (23 ¼″×13 ³⁄₁₆″)
Quilt thread...Dark yellow

Finished size...59cm×33.5cm (23 ¼″×13 ³⁄₁₆″)

☆Seam allowance is indicated in ( )

51cm(20¹⁄₁₆″)

Batting...1 piece   no seam allowance
(seam is 1cm (⅜″))

33.5cm (13³⁄₁₆″)

Lining...Light olive green 1 piece

59cm(23 ¼″)

8cm(3 ⅛″)

(seam is 1cm (⅜″))
Selvage fabric...Green print

A=51cm(20″) B=33.5cm(13 ³⁄₁₆″)
2 pieces each

Patchwork fabric
(Refer to picture)
a=3 pieces b=8pieces c=4 pieces
☆seam allowance is 0.6cm (¼″)

25.5cm (10¹⁄₁₆″)   a

9cm (3⁹⁄₁₆″)   b
9cm(3⁹⁄₁₆″)

6.4cm (2 ½″)   c   9cm(3⁹⁄₁₆″)

9cm(3⁹⁄₁₆″)   9cm(3⁹⁄₁₆″)   6.4cm(2 ½″)

d=8 pieces g=8 pieces
e=32 pieces h=8 pieces
f=32 pieces
Put ⒷB on h, slip stitch and appliqué.

3cm (1³⁄₁₆″) 3cm (1³⁄₁₆″) 3cm (1³⁄₁₆″)

d   e   f   3cm (1³⁄₁₆″)

9cm (3⁹⁄₁₆″)   g   6cm (2³⁄₈″)
1cm(⅜″)

i   h

9cm(3⁹⁄₁₆″)

③Add selvage in order A and B.

④Fold seam allowance of both edges and blind stitch.

Selvage fabric

② Blind stitch on back.
① Sew with right sides together.
Lining   (Patchwork side)

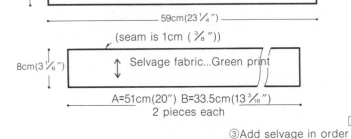

A

c   b

B   a   B

A

4cm(1⁹⁄₁₆″)   4cm(1⁹⁄₁₆″)

①Patchwork.
②Layer batting and lining and quilt.

⟨COASTERS⟩

Materials(for 1)

Green print cotton...32cm(12⁹⁄₁₆″) square (including appliqué fabric)
Light olive green cotton 10.2cm(4″) square
Putchwork fabric (Refer to picture)
Quilt batting 10.2cm(4″) square

Finished size... 10.2(4″)cm square

☆No seam allowance needed.

2.4cm (¹⁵⁄₁₆″)
Bias strip...Print (for 1)
43cm(16¹⁵⁄₁₆″)

*Use pieces d to ⒷB from table center for patchwork fabric, cut batting and lining (Light olive green) 10.2cm(4″) square.

② Blind stitch on back.

Make it round at corner.

①Patchwork.
0.6cm(¼″)

Bias strip
②Layer batting and lining and piping in bias strip.
(Patchwork side)
① Sew with right sides together.

Kitchen
HEART-SHAPED BAG
page 25

Materials
Pink shirting 40cm×35cm(15 ¾″×13 ¾″)
Check, stripe, print cotton (Refer to picture)
Quilt batting 15cm(6″) square
Cardboard 15cm(6″) square
Synthetic cotton
Button (Refer to picture) 1

Finished size...
Bottom...15cm(6″) diameter
Depth...5.5cm(2 3/16″)

Cutting Diagram (actual size)
☆Seam is 0.7cm(¼ ″)

☆Seam allowance is 2cm(¾ ″).

Outer fabric Lining Pink 1 each

Quilt batting ⎫ 1 each
Cardboard ⎭ [Cut 15cm(6″) diameter]

15cm (6″)

Bottom

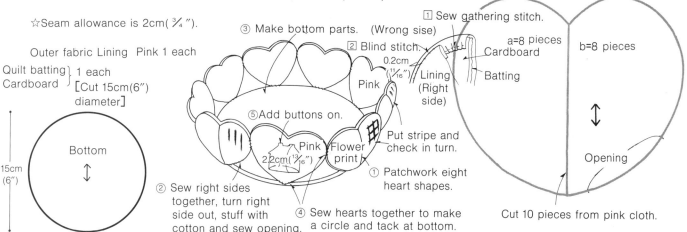

③ Make bottom parts.   (Wrong sise)
① Sew gathering stitch.
② Blind stitch.
0.2cm (1/16 ″)
Pink
a=8 pieces Cardboard
b=8 pieces
Batting
Lining (Right side)
⑤Add buttons on.
Put stripe and check in turn.
Opening
Pink 2.2cm(13/16 ″)
Pink Flower print
① Patchwork eight heart shapes.
② Sew right sides together, turn right side out, stuff with cotton and sew opening.
④ Sew hearts together to make a circle and tack at bottom.
Cut 10 pieces from pink cloth.

Kitchen
TOASTER COVER
page 4.5

Materials
Offwhite quilt fabric 55cm×40cm(21 1/16″×15 ¾″)
Check cotton 65cm×50cm(23 5/8″×19 1/16″)
Patchwork fabric 20cm(7 7/8″) each
(Refer to picture)

Quilt thread...Offwhite
#25 embroidery floss...Blue
Finished size...40cm×55cm
(15 ¾ ″×21 1/16 ″)

☆Seam allowance is indicated in ( )

40cm(15 ¾ ″)
(seam is 1cm (3/8 ″))

←→no seam allowance needed.

Lining...Check 1 piece

Outer fabric...Quilting fabric 1 piece

↔

63cm (24 7/8 ″)

55cm(21 5/8 ″)

48cm(18 7/8 ″)

Patchwork fabric
☆Seam allowance is 0.8cm(5/16 ″)
a.b=8 pieces each

4cm(1 9/16 ″)
↕
←4cm→ (1 9/16 ″)

4cm (1 9/16 ″)   4cm(1 9/16 ″) Ⓐ
Ⓑ   Ⓑ
④Put outer fabric on center of lining. Blind stitch in order Ⓐ Ⓑ

①Embroider on quilt fabric.
Cooking
9cm (3 9/16 ″)
1cm (3/8 ″)
a
b
8cm(3 1/8 ″)
Ⓐ
4cm(1 9/16 ″) 4cm(1 9/16 ″)

②Patchwork.   ③Put it on quilt fabric and quilt.

EMBROIDERY DIAGRAM IS ON PAGE 19

Easy Living

PATCHWORK FOR EVERYDAY LIVING

Make your patchwork the talk of tea time

TABLE CLOTH AND CHAIR CUSHIONS

Instructions on page 30

The table cloth and cushions will give an elegant touch to your dining area. The smooth cotton will make this table cloth your favorite one.

[ACTUAL SIZE]
This patchwork is used for the table cloth and chair cushions.

Living
TABLECLOTH AND CHAIR CUSHIONS
page 28.29

⟨TABLE CLOTH⟩
Materials
Light green polka dots cotton...90cm×172cm(35 $\frac{7}{16}$ ″×67 $\frac{1}{4}$ ″)
(including patchwork fabric)
White cotton...90cm×263cm(35 $\frac{7}{16}$ ″×103 $\frac{1}{2}$ ″) (including patchwork fabric)
Light green check cotton...90cm×170cm(35 $\frac{7}{16}$ ″×67″)
Pink polka dots print...40cm×35cm(15 $\frac{3}{4}$ ″×13 $\frac{3}{4}$ ″)
Green flower pattern print...40cm(15 $\frac{3}{4}$ ″) square
Thin quilt batting...90cm×263cm(35 $\frac{7}{16}$ ″×103 $\frac{1}{2}$ ″)
Quilt thread...Offwhite
Finished size...131.4cm(51 $\frac{3}{4}$ ″)square

☆Seam allowance is indicated in ( )

(seam is 1cm($\frac{3}{8}$ ″))
48cm (18 $\frac{7}{8}$ ″)
Center fabric
Light green polka dots 1 piece
48cm(18 $\frac{7}{8}$ ″)

*Lining (White cotton)
Join 90cm×131.4cm (35 $\frac{7}{16}$ ″×51 $\frac{3}{4}$ ″) and 44cm×131.4cm (17 $\frac{5}{16}$ ″×51 $\frac{3}{4}$ ″) pieces together with 1.3cm($\frac{1}{2}$ ″) seam allowance and make 131.4cm(15 $\frac{3}{4}$ ″) square.
*Quilt batting
Overcast 90cm×131.4cm(35 $\frac{7}{16}$ ″×51 $\frac{3}{4}$ ″) and 41.4cm×131.4cm (16 $\frac{1}{4}$ ″×51 $\frac{3}{4}$ ″) and join pieces, make 131.4cm(51 $\frac{3}{4}$ ″) square

Bias strip Check 1 piece

2.8cm(1 $\frac{1}{8}$ ″)
(no seam allowance needed)
530cm(208″) (Join pieces)

(seam is 1 cm ($\frac{3}{8}$ ″))
Border strip a Light green polka dots 2 pieces
80cm (31 $\frac{1}{2}$ ″)
20cm (7 $\frac{7}{8}$ ″)

(seam is 1 cm ($\frac{3}{8}$ ″))
Border strip b Light green polka dots 2 pieces
120cm (47 $\frac{1}{4}$ ″)
20cm (7 $\frac{7}{8}$ ″)

(seam is 1 cm ($\frac{3}{8}$ ″))
Border strip c Check 2 pieces
120cm (47 $\frac{1}{4}$ ″)
5cm(2″)

(seam is 1 cm ($\frac{3}{8}$ ″))
Border strip d Check 2 pieces
130cm (51 $\frac{3}{16}$ ″)
5cm(2″)

① Sew with right sides together.
② Blind stitch to back.
0.7cm($\frac{5}{16}$ ″)
(Right side)
⑧Piping around by bias strip.
0.7cm($\frac{5}{16}$ ″)

⑥Sew border strip on⑤ in order c.d with right sides together.

Border strip c
Border strip a
①Patchwork and make blocks A~D.

A B C D F
G
E
Center fabric
Border strip b
Border strip d

⑤Sew border strip on④ in order a.b with right sides together.

③Join A~D block pieces with F and G cloth.

②Make block E and appliqué on center by slip stitch.

④Sew ③ and center cloth with right sides together.

130cm (51 $\frac{3}{16}$ ″)

0.7cm($\frac{5}{16}$ ″)

⑦Layer quilt batting and lining (Join pieces 131.4cm(51 $\frac{3}{4}$ ″) square each) and quilt except for patchwork stitches place.

Patchwork fabric
(Refer to picture)
☆Seam allowance is 0.8cm($\frac{5}{16}$ ″)

a.b= 16 pieces each
a.b.f= 4 pieces each
c.d.e= 8 pieces each

16cm (6 $\frac{1}{4}$ ″)
a b
8cm (3 $\frac{1}{8}$ ″)
8cm (3 $\frac{1}{8}$ ″)

a
d c b
e
f

16cm(6 $\frac{1}{4}$ ″)

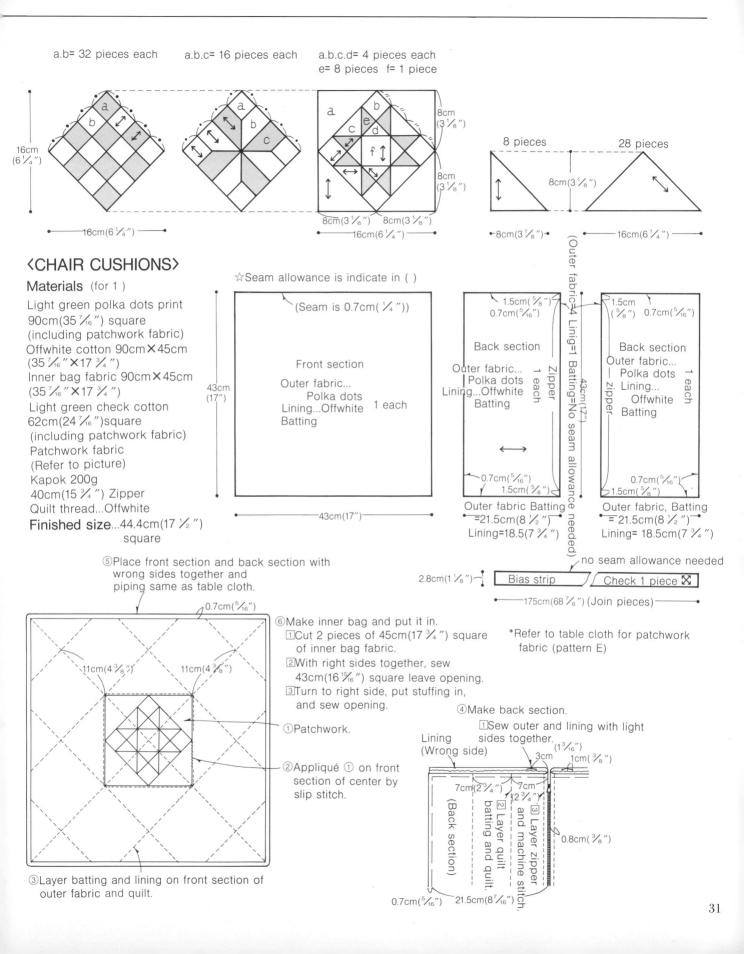

a.b= 32 pieces each   a.b.c= 16 pieces each   a.b.c.d= 4 pieces each
e= 8 pieces f= 1 piece

16cm (6¼")

16cm(6¼")

a
b

a
b
c

a
b
c
e
d
f

8cm(3⅛")
8cm(3⅛")

8cm(3⅛") 8cm(3⅛")

16cm(6¼")

8 pieces   28 pieces

8cm(3⅛")

8cm(3⅛")   16cm(6¼")

‹CHAIR CUSHIONS›

Materials (for 1)

Light green polka dots print 90cm(35⁷⁄₁₆") square (including patchwork fabric)
Offwhite cotton 90cm×45cm (35⁷⁄₁₆"×17¾")
Inner bag fabric 90cm×45cm (35⁷⁄₁₆"×17¾")
Light green check cotton 62cm(24⁷⁄₁₆")square (including patchwork fabric)
Patchwork fabric (Refer to picture)
Kapok 200g
40cm(15¾") Zipper
Quilt thread...Offwhite

Finished size...44.4cm(17½") square

☆Seam allowance is indicate in ( )

(Seam is 0.7cm(¼"))

Front section

Outer fabric...
   Polka dots
Lining...Offwhite
Batting   1 each

43cm (17")

43cm(17")

1.5cm(⅝")
0.7cm(⁵⁄₁₆")

Back section
Outer fabric...
   Polka dots
Lining...Offwhite
Batting

1 each
zipper

0.7cm(⁵⁄₁₆")
1.5cm(⅝")

Outer fabric Batting
=21.5cm(8½")
Lining=18.5(7¾")

1.5cm (⅝") 0.7cm(⁵⁄₁₆")

Back section
Outer fabric...
   Polka dots
Lining...
   Offwhite
Batting

1 each
zipper

0.7cm(⁵⁄₁₆")
1.5cm(⅝")

Outer fabric, Batting
=21.5cm(8½")
Lining= 18.5cm(7¾")

(Outer fabric=4 Linig=1 Batting=No seam allowance needed)

43cm (12")

no seam allowance needed

2.8cm(1⅛")

Bias strip   Check 1 piece ⊠

175cm(68⅞") (Join pieces)

⑤Place front section and back section with wrong sides together and piping same as table cloth.

0.7cm(⁵⁄₁₆")

11cm(4⅜")   11cm(4⅜")

①Patchwork.

②Appliqué ① on front section of center by slip stitch.

③Layer batting and lining on front section of outer fabric and quilt.

⑥Make inner bag and put it in.
  ① Cut 2 pieces of 45cm(17¾") square of inner bag fabric.
  ② With right sides together, sew 43cm(16¹⁵⁄₁₆") square leave opening.
  ③ Turn to right side, put stuffing in, and sew opening.

④Make back section.
  ① Sew outer and lining with light sides together.

*Refer to table cloth for patchwork fabric (pattern E)

Lining (Wrong side)

3cm   (1³⁄₁₆")
1cm(⅜")

7cm (2¾")   7cm (2¾")

(Back section)

① Layer quilt batting and machine stitch.
② Layer quilt batting and quilt.
③ Layer zipper and machine stitch.

0.8cm(⅜")

0.7cm(⁵⁄₁₆") 21.5cm(8⁷⁄₁₆")

Living
PILLOWS
Instructions on page 34
Make a pillow on warm, sunny day.
Each pattern will build your skills.

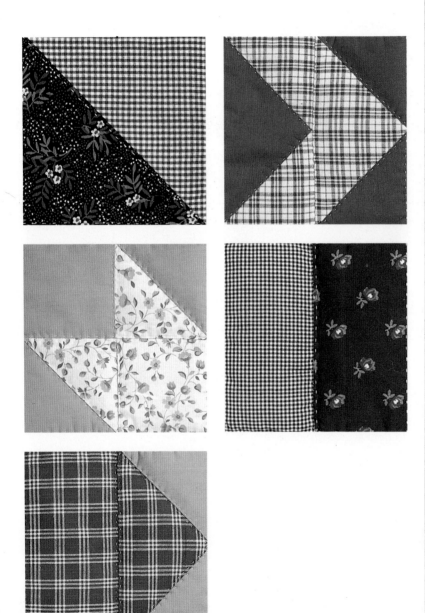

5 different patterns you can make easily.

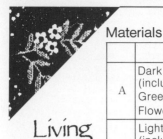

Materials

	Cotton	Common
A	Dark green plain fabric...80cm×50cm(31 ½ ″×19 ¹¹⁄₁₆ ″) (including patchwork fabric) Green check...60cm×40cm(23 ⅝ ″×15 ¾ ″) Flower pattern print...17cm(6 ¹¹⁄₁₆ ″) square	Inner fabric cotton...47cm(18 ½ ″) square Quilt batting...47cm(18 ½ ″) square 40cm(15 ¾ ″) Zipper 45cm(17 ¾ ″) square cushion Quilt thread...Offwhite
B	Light green plain fabric 85cm×50cm(33 ½ ″×19 ¹¹⁄₁₆ ″) (including patchwork fabric) Flower pattern print 40cm×35cm(15 ¾ ″×13 ¾ ″) Green check...70cm×25cm(27 ½ ″×10″)	
C	Blue plain fabric...90cm×50cm(35 ⁷⁄₁₆ ″×19 ¹¹⁄₁₆ ″) Patchwork fabric...12cm(4 ¾ ″)square each (Refer to piecture)	
D	Flower print on blue...90cm×60cm(35 ⁷⁄₁₆ ″×23 ⅝ ″) (including patchwork fabric) Print on offwhite fabric, Blue check...24cm(9 ½ ″) square each	
E	Blue check...70cm×50cm(27 ½ ″×19 ¹¹⁄₁₆ ″) (including patchwork fabric) Flower print on white...55cm×50cm(21 ¹¹⁄₁₆ ″×19 ¹¹⁄₁₆ ″) (including patchwork fabric) Flower print on blue...28cm×12cm(11″×4 ¾ ″)	

Living

PILLOWS
page 32.33

Finished size...45cm(17 ¾ ″) square

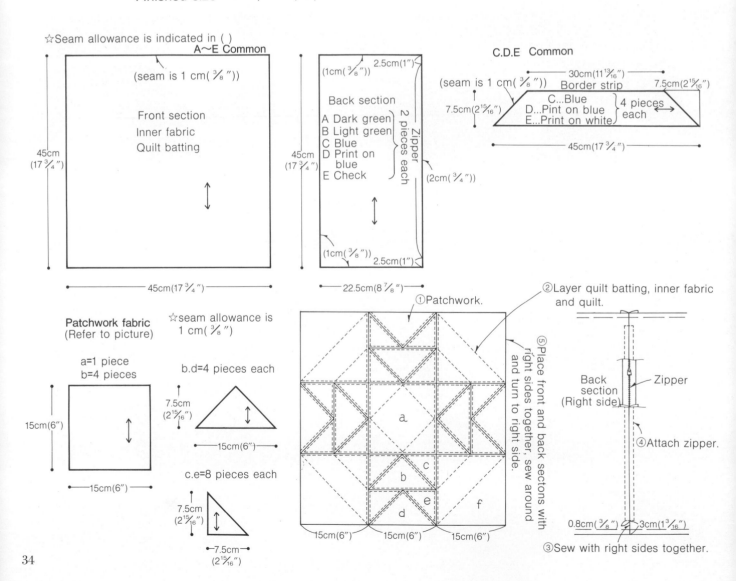

☆Seam allowance is indicated in ( )

A~E Common

(seam is 1 cm(⅜ ″))

Front section
Inner fabric
Quilt batting

45cm
(17 ¾ ″)

45cm(17 ¾ ″)

2.5cm(1″)
(1cm(⅜ ″))

Back section
A Dark green
B Light green
C Blue
D Print on blue
E Check

Zipper
2 pieces each

(2cm(¾ ″))

45cm
(17 ¾ ″)

(1cm(⅜ ″))
2.5cm(1″)

22.5cm(8 ⅞ ″)

C.D.E Common

(seam is 1 cm(⅜ ″))

30cm(11 ¹³⁄₁₆ ″)
Border strip
7.5cm(2 ¹⁵⁄₁₆ ″)

7.5cm(2 ¹⁵⁄₁₆ ″)
C...Blue
D...Pint on blue
E...Print on white
4 pieces each

45cm(17 ¾ ″)

Patchwork fabric
(Refer to picture)

a=1 piece
b=4 pieces

15cm(6″)

15cm(6″)

☆seam allowance is
1 cm(⅜ ″)

b.d=4 pieces each

7.5cm
(2 ¹⁵⁄₁₆ ″)

15cm(6″)

c.e=8 pieces each

7.5cm
(2 ¹⁵⁄₁₆ ″)

7.5cm
(2 ¹⁵⁄₁₆ ″)

①Patchwork.

②Layer quilt batting, inner fabric
and quilt.

a

c
b
e
d
f

15cm(6″) 15cm(6″) 15cm(6″)

⑤Place front and back sections with
right sides together, sew around
and turn to right side.

Back
section
(Right side)

Zipper

④Attach zipper.

0.8cm(⅜ ″) 3cm(1 ³⁄₁₆ ″)

③Sew with right sides together.

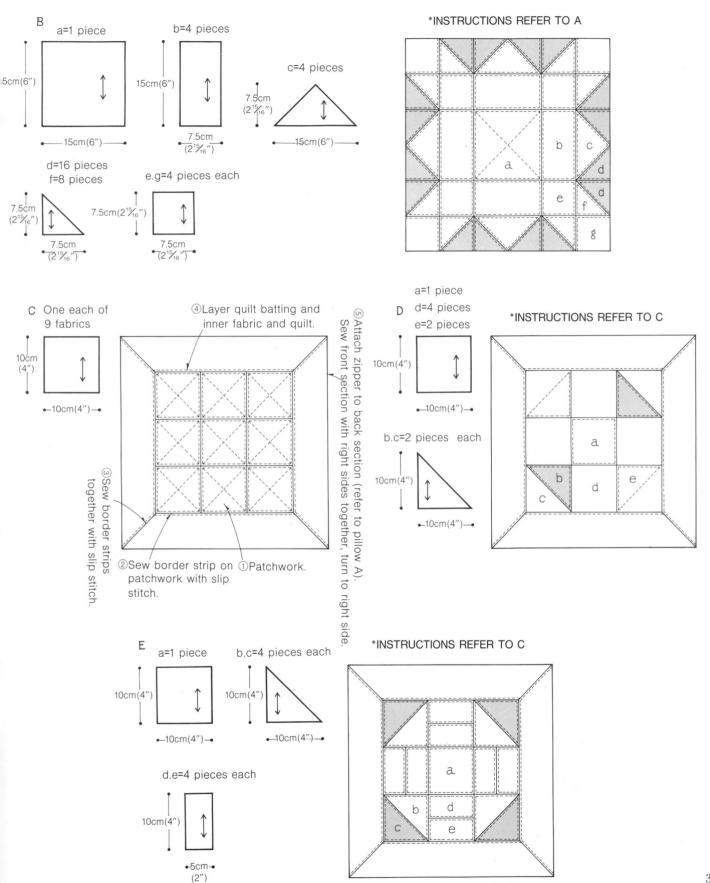

Living
PILLOWS,
FLOOR MAT,
SLIPPERS

Instructions on page 38
Your best friends will feel right at home with these cozy patchwork patterns.

Appliqué patchwork on
ready-made slippers.

FLOOR MAT, PILLOWS, SLIPPERS.
page 36.37

⟨FLOOR MAT⟩

Material

Dark brown corduroy 70cm×122cm(27 ½″×48″)

Blue print cotton 90cm×80cm(35 ½″×31 ½″)

Blue gray print cotton 90cm×70cm(35 ½″×27 ½″)

Brown print cotton 54cm×60cm(21 ¼″×23 ⅝″)

Quilt batting 68cm×120cm(26 ¾″×47 ¼″)

#25 embroidery floss...gray

Nonskid backing 66cm×118cm(26″×46 ½″)

Finished size...120cm×68cm(47 ¼″×26 ¾″)

Patchwork fabric

☆Seam allowance is 1 cm(⅜″) for floor mat, pillows.
 Seam allowance is 0.6cm(¼″) for slippers.
 Indications in ( )is for slippers.
 Floor mat a〜f=32 pieces each (Print and plain= 16 pieces each)
 Slippers(for 1) a〜f=8 pieces each (Print and plain= 4 pieces each)
 Pillows (for 1) a〜f=4 pieces each (Print and plain =2 pieces each)

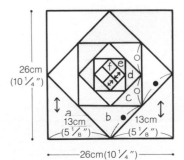

* [] is for slipper.
  Floor mat and pillows unless indicated otherwise

☆Seam allowance is 1 cm(⅜″)

68cm (26 ¾″) | Opening

Lining...Corduroy
Quilt batting... } 1 each
[no seam needed]

120cm(47 ¼″)

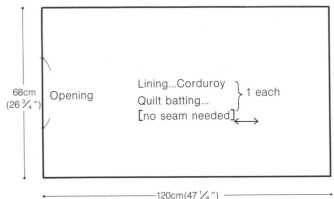

Border strip

Print (Blue)
(10cm (4″)) 2 pieces
8cm(3 ⅛″) A 8cm(3 ⅛″)
26cm (10 ¼″)

Print (Brown)
47cm(18 ½″)
C Symmetry 2 pieces each
39cm(15 ⅜″)

4 pieces
8cm(3 ⅛″) 8cm(3 ⅛″)
8 cm (3 ⅛″)

D 2 pieces
52cm(20 ⁷⁄₁₆″)

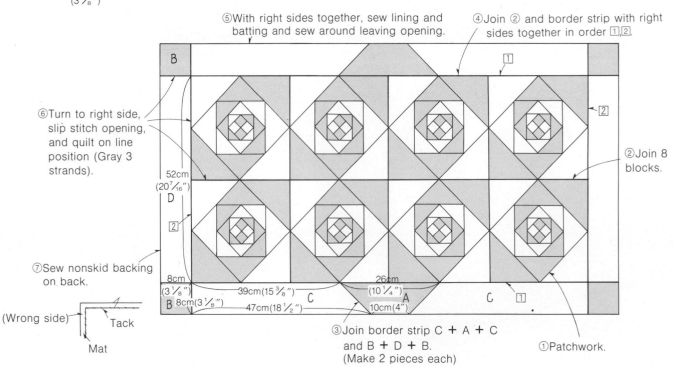

⑤With right sides together, sew lining and batting and sew around leaving opening.

④Join ② and border strip with right sides together in order 1,2.

⑥Turn to right side, slip stitch opening, and quilt on line position (Gray 3 strands).

②Join 8 blocks.

⑦Sew nonskid backing on back.

(Wrong side) Tack Mat

③Join border strip C ＋ A ＋ C and B ＋ D ＋ B. (Make 2 pieces each)

①Patchwork.

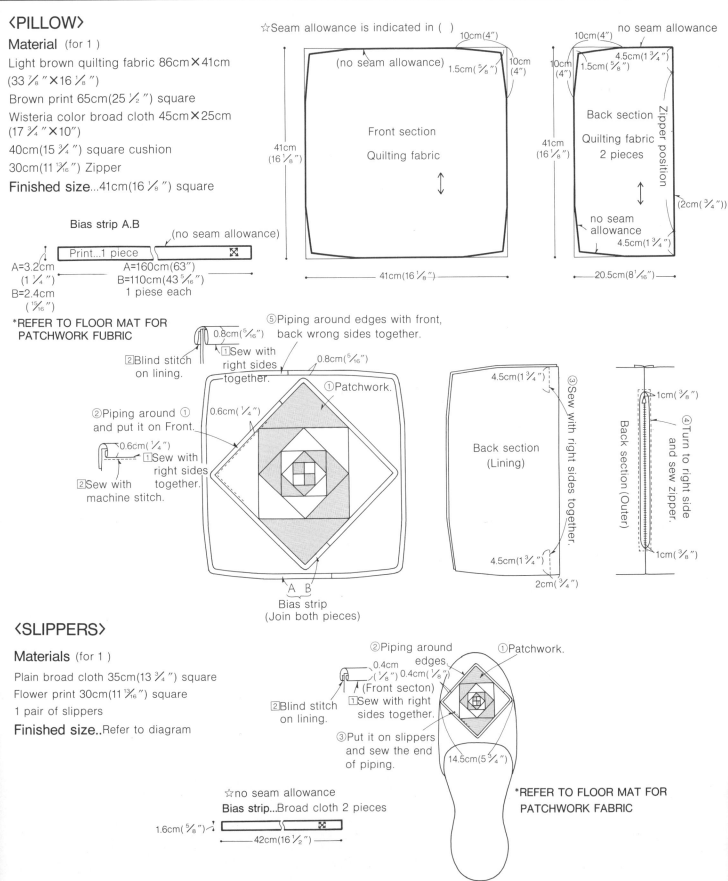

⟨PILLOW⟩

Material (for 1)

Light brown quilting fabric 86cm×41cm
(33 ⅞″×16 ⅛″)

Brown print 65cm(25 ½″) square

Wisteria color broad cloth 45cm×25cm
(17 ¾″×10″)

40cm(15 ¾″) square cushion

30cm(11 ¹³⁄₁₆″) Zipper

Finished size...41cm(16 ⅛″) square

Bias strip A.B

(no seam allowance)

Print...1 piece

A=3.2cm
(1 ¼″)
A=160cm(63″)
B=2.4cm
(¹⁵⁄₁₆″)
B=110cm(43 ⁵⁄₁₆″)
1 piese each

*REFER TO FLOOR MAT FOR
PATCHWORK FUBRIC

☆Seam allowance is indicated in ( )

10cm(4″)   no seam allowance

(no seam allowance)   1.5cm(⁵⁄₈″)   10cm(4″)

10cm(4″)   4.5cm(1 ¾″)   1.5cm(⁵⁄₈″)

41cm
(16 ⅛″)

Front section
Quilting fabric

Back section
Quilting fabric
2 pieces

Zipper position

no seam
allowance

4.5cm(1 ¾″)

(2cm(¾″))

41cm(16 ⅛″)   20.5cm(8¹⁄₁₆″)

⑤Piping around edges with front,
back wrong sides together.

0.8cm(⁵⁄₁₆″)

①Sew with
right sides
together.

②Blind stitch
on lining.

0.8cm(⁵⁄₁₆″)

②Piping around ①
and put it on Front.

①Patchwork.

0.6cm(¼″)

0.6cm(¼″)
①Sew with
right sides
together.

②Sew with
machine stitch.

A B

Bias strip
(Join both pieces)

4.5cm(1 ¾″)

Back section
(Lining)

③Sew with right sides together.

4.5cm(1 ¾″)

2cm(¾″)

1cm(⅜″)

④Turn to right side
and sew zipper.

Back section (Outer)

1cm(⅜″)

⟨SLIPPERS⟩

Materials (for 1)

Plain broad cloth 35cm(13 ¾″) square

Flower print 30cm(11 ¹³⁄₁₆″) square

1 pair of slippers

Finished size..Refer to diagram

②Piping around
edges.

①Patchwork.

0.4cm
(⅛″)   0.4cm (⅛″)

(Front secton)

②Blind stitch
on lining.

①Sew with right
sides together.

③Put it on slippers
and sew the end
of piping.

14.5cm(5 ¾″)

☆no seam allowance

Bias strip...Broad cloth 2 pieces

1.6cm(⅝″)

42cm(16 ½″)

*REFER TO FLOOR MAT FOR
PATCHWORK FABRIC

Living
PICTURE FRAME
Instruction on page 42

You'll enjoy this cozy tree and house pattern patchwork

40

[ACTUAL SIZE] Embroidery and Appliqué

Living
ORNAMENTS

Instructions on page 43
TISSUE BOX COVER

Instruction on page 42
Good idear that go perfectly with any room.

Heart shape patchwork ornament.

Living
PICTURE FRAME
page 40

Materials

Olive green cotton 40cm×25cm(15 ¾ "×10")

White cotton 20cm(7 ⅞ ") squre

Check, Cream, Stripe cotton

Print for appliqué

Quilt batting 24cm(9 ½ ") square

#25 embroidery floss...Yellow

Quilt thread...Offwhite

20cm(7 ⅞ ") inside diameter square frame strip

Finished size...Same as frame

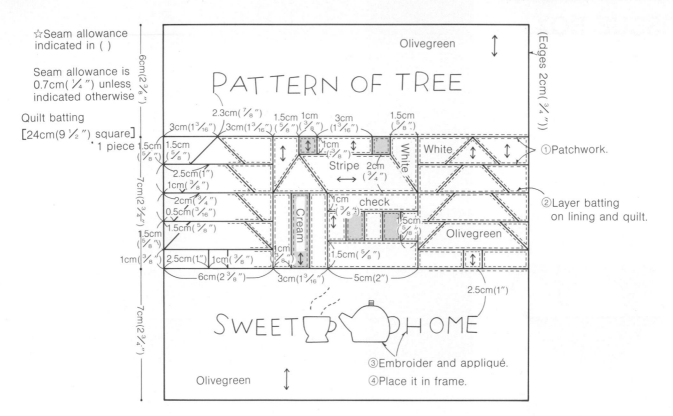

☆Seam allowance indicated in ( )

Seam allowance is 0.7cm(¼ ") unless indicated otherwise

Quilt batting [24cm(9 ½ ") square] 1 piece

① Patchwork.

② Layer batting on lining and quilt.

③ Embroider and appliqué.

④ Place it in frame.

EMBROIDERY AND APPLIQUÉ DIAGRAM [ACTUAL SIZE]

☆Embroidery 2 strands

☆Seam allowance is 0.5cm(3⁄16 ") for appliqué fabric and appliqué by slip stitch.

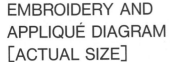

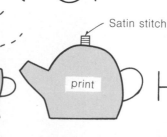

Living
TISSUE BOX COVER
page 41

Materials

Pink quilt fabric 41cm×31cm(16 ⅛ "×12 ¼ ")

Patchwork, Appliqué fabric (Refer to picture)

1.6cm(⅝ ") wide bias strip 80cm(31 ½ ")

0.8cm(5⁄16 ") wide rubber tape 14cm(5 ½ ")

#25 embroidery floss...Deep red

Quilt thread...Offwhite

Synthetic cotton

Finished size...25cm×8.5cm×12c

(10"×3 5⁄16 "×4 ¾ ")

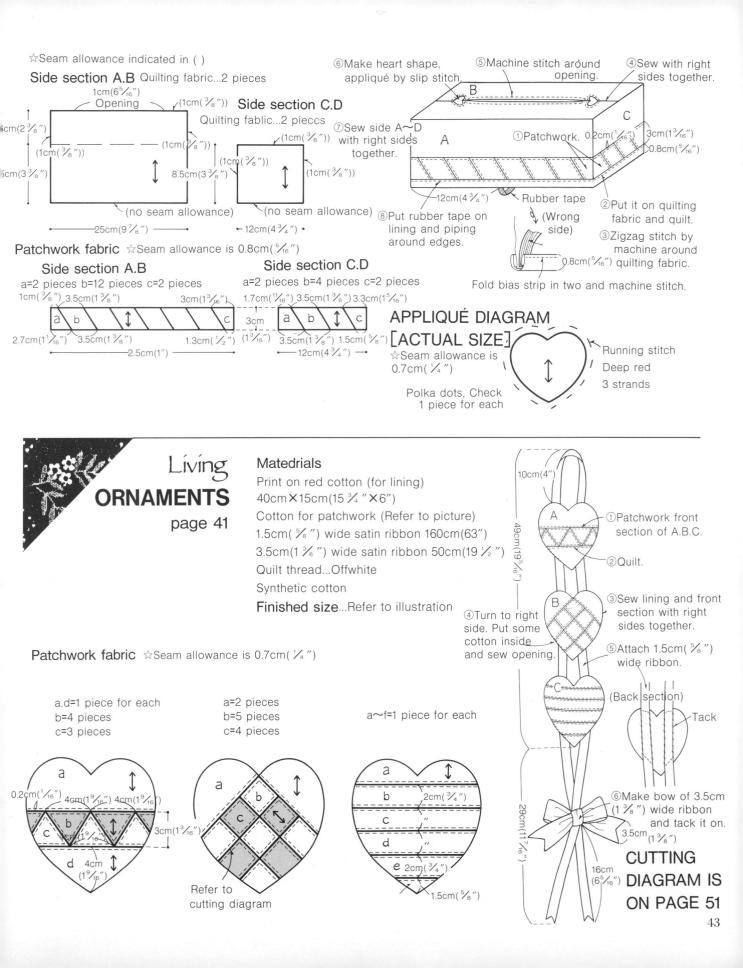

☆Seam allowance indicated in ( )

Side section A.B Quilting fabric...2 pieces

1cm(6⁵⁄₁₆")
Opening
(1cm(³⁄₈"))
3cm(2³⁄₈")
(1cm(³⁄₈"))
5cm(3³⁄₈")
(1cm(³⁄₈"))
8.5cm(3³⁄₈")
(no seam allowance)
25cm(9⁷⁄₈")

Side section C.D
Quilting fablic...2 pieces

(1cm(³⁄₈"))
(1cm(³⁄₈"))
(1cm(³⁄₈"))
(no seam allowance)
12cm(4³⁄₄")

⑥Make heart shape, appliqué by slip stitch.
⑤Machine stitch around opening.
④Sew with right sides together.

⑦Sew side A~D with right sides together.

①Patchwork. 0.2cm(¹⁄₁₆")
3cm(1³⁄₁₆")
0.8cm(⁵⁄₁₆")

②Put it on quilting fabric and quilt.

③Zigzag stitch by machine around 0.8cm(⁵⁄₁₆") quilting fabric.

⑧Put rubber tape on lining and piping around edges.

12cm(4³⁄₄")
Rubber tape
(Wrong side)
Fold bias strip in two and machine stitch.

Patchwork fabric ☆Seam allowance is 0.8cm(⁵⁄₁₆")

Side section A.B
a=2 pieces b=12 pieces c=2 pieces

1cm(³⁄₈") 3.5cm(1³⁄₈")   3cm(1³⁄₁₆")
a b   c
2.7cm(1¹⁄₁₆") 3.5cm(1³⁄₈")   1.3cm(¹⁄₂")
2.5cm(1")

Side section C.D
a=2 pieces b=4 pieces c=2 pieces

1.7cm(¹¹⁄₁₆") 3.5cm(1³⁄₈") 3.3cm(1⁵⁄₁₆")
a b c
3cm(1³⁄₁₆")
3.5cm(1³⁄₈") 1.5cm(⁵⁄₈")
12cm(4³⁄₄")

APPLIQUÉ DIAGRAM [ACTUAL SIZE]
☆Seam allowance is 0.7cm(¹⁄₄")

Polka dots, Check
1 piece for each

Running stitch
Deep red
3 strands

Living ORNAMENTS
page 41

Matedrials
Print on red cotton (for lining)
40cm×15cm(15¾"×6")
Cotton for patchwork (Refer to picture)
1.5cm(⁵⁄₈") wide satin ribbon 160cm(63")
3.5cm(1³⁄₈") wide satin ribbon 50cm(19½")
Quilt thread...Offwhite
Synthetic cotton
Finished size...Refer to illustration

10cm(4")
A
①Patchwork front section of A.B.C.
②Quilt.
B
③Sew lining and front section with right sides together.
49cm(19⁵⁄₁₆")
④Turn to right side. Put some cotton inside and sew opening.
⑤Attach 1.5cm(⁵⁄₈") wide ribbon.
(Back section)
C
Tack
⑥Make bow of 3.5cm(1³⁄₈") wide ribbon and tack it on.
3.5cm(1³⁄₈")
29cm(11⁷⁄₁₆")
16cm(6⁵⁄₁₆")

Patchwork fabric ☆Seam allowance is 0.7cm(¹⁄₄")

a.d=1 piece for each
b=4 pieces
c=3 pieces

a=2 pieces
b=5 pieces
c=4 pieces

a~f=1 piece for each

a
0.2cm(¹⁄₁₆")
4cm(1⁹⁄₁₆") 4cm(1⁹⁄₁₆")
b
c
3cm(1³⁄₁₆")
d 4cm (1⁹⁄₁₆")

a
b
c
Refer to cutting diagram

a
b 2cm(¾")
c "
d "
e 2cm(¾")
1.5cm(⁵⁄₈")

CUTTING DIAGRAM IS ON PAGE 51

[ACTUAL SIZE]
Patchwork is called
Grandms's flower patch

Living

SOFA COVER & PILLOWS

Instructions on page 46

100% cotton color prints add a wonderful accent to your patchwork.
Always gives a cozy touch to your living room.

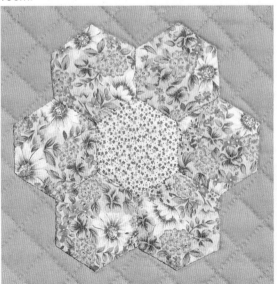

Living
SOFA COVER
& PILLOWS
page 44,45

⟨SOFA COVER⟩
Materials

Yellow cotton 90cm×306cm
(35 ½″×120 ½″)

Offwhite cotton 88cm(34 ⅝″)square

Flower print cotton 88cm×66cm(34 ⅝″×26″)

Cotton for patchwork 30cm×20cm
(11 ¹³⁄₁₆″×7 ⅞″)each

Finished size...128cm(50 ⅜″)square

☆Seam allowance indicated in ( )

140cm(55 ⅛″)

Fold line

Lining   Yellow
         2 pieces

(seam 1cm(⅜″))

6cm(2⅜″)

70cm(27⁹⁄₁₆″)

Outer fabric

a=20 pieces
b=4 pieces } Yellow

c=13 pieces...Offwhite
d=12 pieces...Print

20cm(7⅞″)   a   (seam 1cm(⅜″))

4cm(1⁹⁄₁₆″)

116cm(45¹¹⁄₁₆″)   b   (seam 1cm(⅜″))

4cm(1⁹⁄₁₆″)

20cm(7⅞″)   c、d   (seam 1cm(⅜″))

20cm(7⅞″)

Patchwork fabric

Seam allowance
is 0.8cm(⁵⁄₁₆″)

7 kinds of fabrics=
13 pieces each

5cm(2″)

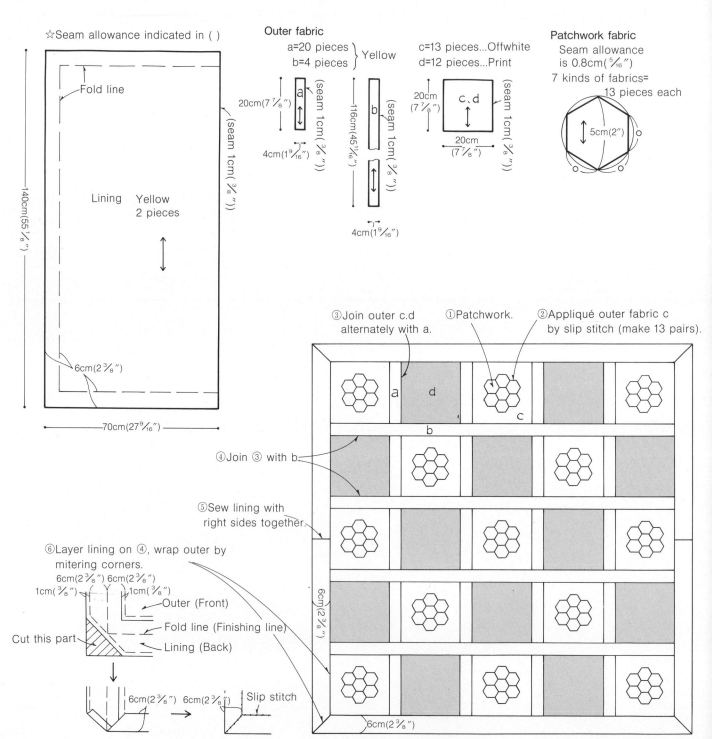

③Join outer c.d
alternately with a.

①Patchwork.

②Appliqué outer fabric c
by slip stitch (make 13 pairs).

④Join ③ with b.

⑤Sew lining with
right sides together.

⑥Layer lining on ④, wrap outer by
mitering corners.

6cm(2⅜″) 6cm(2⅜″)
1cm(⅜″)   1cm(⅜″)
Outer (Front)
Fold line (Finishing line)
Cut this part
Lining (Back)

6cm(2⅜″) 6cm(2⅜″) Slip stitch

a   d
b
c

6cm(2⅜″)

6cm(2⅜″)

⟨PILLOWS⟩

Materials...45cm(17 ¾ ")square

[ ] is pink,use same color unless indicated otherwise

Green [Pink] coton...53cm×94cm(20 ⅞ "×37")

Small flower print cotton [branch print cotton]
55cm×11cm(21 1/16 "×4 ⅜ ")

Small flower print on yellow cotton [Flower print on gray cotton]
30cm×20cm(11 13/16 "×7 ⅞ ")

Inner fabric cotton 47cm(18 ½ ")square

Quilt batting 47cm(18 ½ ")square

30cm(11 13/16 ")Zipper

Quilt thread...Offwhite

45cm(17 ¾ ")square cushion

☆Seam allowance indicated in ( )
[ ] is pink,use same color unless indicated
otherwise

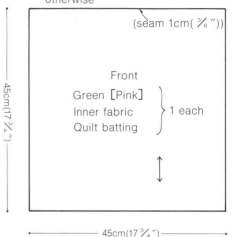

(seam 1cm(⅜ "))

45cm(17 ¾ ")

Front
Green [Pink]
Inner fabric } 1 each
Quilt batting

45cm(17 ¾ ")

Finished size...45cm(17 ¾ ")square

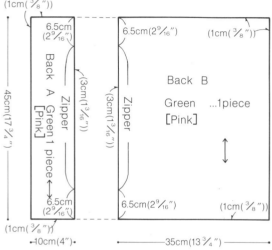

(1cm(⅜ "))
6.5cm (2 9/16 ")
Back A Green 1 piece [Pink]
(3cm(1 3/16 "))
Zipper
6.5cm (2 9/16 ")
(1cm(⅜ "))
10cm(4")

6.5cm(2 9/16 ")
Back B
Green ...1piece [Pink]
(3cm(1 3/16 "))
Zipper
6.5cm(2 9/16 ")
(1cm(⅜ "))
45cm(17 ¾ ")
35cm(13 ¾ ")

Decoration fabric
Small flower print [Branch print] 4 pieces

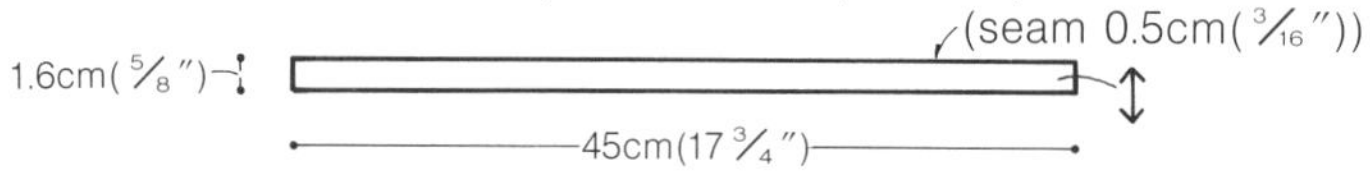

1.6cm(⅝ ")

(seam 0.5cm(³⁄₁₆ "))

45cm(17 ¾ ")

Patchwork fabric (Refer to picture)
☆seam allowance is 0.9cm(⅜ ")

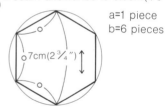

a=1 piece
b=6 pieces

7cm(2 ¾ ")

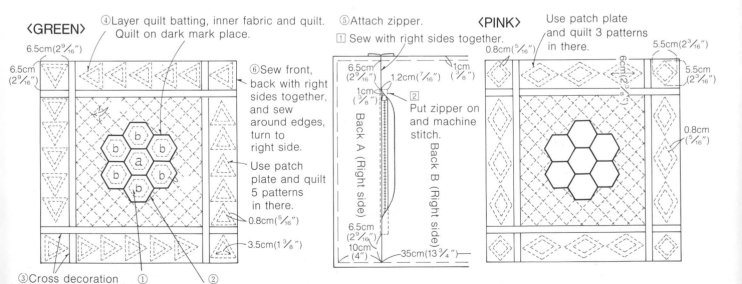

⟨GREEN⟩

④Layer quilt batting, inner fabric and quilt.
Quilt on dark mark place.

⑤Attach zipper.
① Sew with right sides together.

⟨PINK⟩

Use patch plate
and quilt 3 patterns
in there.

6.5cm(2 9/16 ")
6.5cm (2 9/16 ")

⑥Sew front,
back with right
sides together,
and sew
around edges,
turn to
right side.

Use patch
plate and quilt
5 patterns
in there.

0.8cm(⁵⁄₁₆ ")

3.5cm(1 ⅜ ")

③Cross decoration
fabric and appliqué
by slip stitch.

① Patchwork.

② Appliqué on
outer fabric by slip stitch.

6.5cm (2 9/16 ")
1cm (⅜ ")
1.2cm(⁷⁄₁₆ ")
1cm (⅜ ")
② Put zipper on
and machine
stitch.
Back A (Right side)
Back B (Right side)
6.5cm (2 9/16 ")
10cm (4")
35cm(13 ¾ ")

0.8cm(⁵⁄₁₆ ")
5.5cm(2 ³⁄₁₆ ")
6cm(2 ⅜ ")
5.5cm (2 ³⁄₁₆ ")
0.8cm (⁵⁄₁₆ ")

Living
WALL HANGING
LITTLE BASKET

Instructions on page 50

Hand made! I love it!

Patchwork for those who love red choose your favorite fabric.

[ACTUAL SIZE] Wall hanging patchwork pattern using many shades of red.

[ACTUAL SIZE] Little patchwork basket.

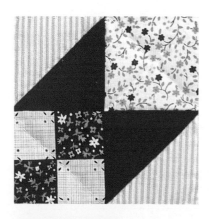

Pink stripes for the inside of the basket.

48

Living
WALL HANGING
page 48·49

Materials
White polka dots cotton 60cm×50cm
(23 ⅝″×19 ¹¹⁄₁₆″) (including patchwork fabric)
Cotton for patchwork (Refer to picture)
2.5cm(1″)wide cotton tape 68cm(26 ¾″)
Quilt batting 44cm(17 ⁵⁄₁₆″)square

Quilt thread...Offwhite, Red
Finished size... Refer to illustration

☆Seam allowance in ( )

Fold line
2cm(¾″)

2cm(³⁄₄″)

48cm(18⅞″)

(seam 1cm(³⁄₈″))

Lining...Polka dots
Quilt batting [Cut44cm (17⁵⁄₁₆″) square] } 1 each

48cm(18⅞″)

④Make casing.

Fold in half of 17cm(6¹⁄₁₆″) lace and tack.

0.3 cm (⅛″)

Ⓑ 4.5cm (1¾″)

0.5 cm (³⁄₁₆″) (Wrong side)

44cm(17⁵⁄₁₆″)

44cm(17⁵⁄₁₆″)

Ⓐ   Ⓐ

Ⓑ

0.2cm (¹⁄₁₆″)

2cm(³⁄₄″)

2cm (¾″)

2 1cm cm (³⁄₄″) (³⁄₈″)

①Patchwork and join pieces.

②Layer batting on back and quilt. (Use red thread for red color of fabrics, offwhite thread for light color fabrics.

③Put front on center of lining, fold in two in order Ⓐ Ⓑ and blind stitch.

Quilt batting

Lining (Wrong side)

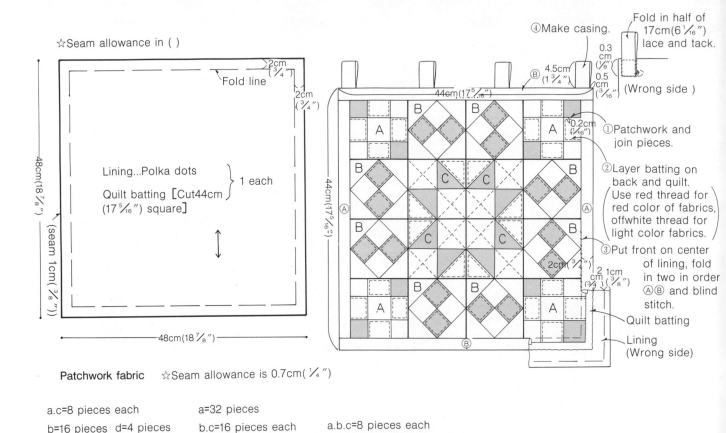

Patchwork fabric   ☆Seam allowance is 0.7cm(¼″)

a.c=8 pieces each
b=16 pieces   d=4 pieces

a	b	c
	d	

3cm(1³⁄₁₆″)
4cm(1⁹⁄₁₆″)
3cm(1³⁄₁₆″)

3cm (1³⁄₁₆″)   4cm (1⁹⁄₁₆″)   3cm (1³⁄₁₆″)

a=32 pieces
b.c=16 pieces each

5cm(2″)
5cm(2″)

a
b
c

5cm (2″)   5cm (2″)

a.b.c=8 pieces each

5cm(2″)
5cm(2″)

a   c
b

5cm (2″)   5cm (2″)

Living
LITTLE BASCKET
page 48.49

Materials
Pink stripe cotton 58cm×28cm
(22 ¹³⁄₁₆″×11″)
Pink quilting fabric 19cm(7 ½″)square
White polka dots cotton 58cm×15cm
(22 ¹³⁄₁₆″×6″)
Print Ⓐ on white cotton 20cm(7 ⅞″)
square
Print on red cotton 15cm×20cm
(6″×7 ⅞″)

Print Ⓑ on white cotton, Check cotton
Quilt batting 56cm×25cm(22″×10″)
Cardboard 17cm(6¹⁄₁₆″)square
Wooded beads 4 pieces 0.6cm(¼″)
in diameter
Synthetic cotton
Finished size... Bottom...17cm(6¹⁄₁₆″)
diameter
Depth...8.5cm(3 ⁵⁄₁₆″)

☆Seam allowance indicated in ( )

Outer fabric...Quilting fabric
Lining...Stripe
Quilt batting ⎫ no seam
Cardboard ⎭ needed

Bottom

17cm(6¹¹⁄₁₆″)

(1cm(³⁄₈″))

Handle
Print on red Print Ⓐ on white 2 pieces each
Quilt batting (no seam nedded) 4 pieces

1 piece for each

18cm(7¹⁄₁₆″)

(seam 1cm(³⁄₈″))

2cm(³⁄₄″)

③Put cotton of each patchwork and sew opening.

④Make handles.

Batting

1cm(³⁄₈″)

Gather stitch of edges.

12cm
(4³⁄₄″)

Put batting, wrap around and blind stitch.

⑤Attach handles and wooden beads.

⑥Gathering stitch around lining of bottom, make bottom layer cardboard and batting, place it inside and press in firmly.

Batting
Border strip   1.5cm(⁵⁄₈″)
① Sew with right sides together.   ② Blind stitch.
4cm 4cm
(1⁹⁄₁₆″)(1⁹⁄₁₆″)
(Wrong side)
Synthetic cotton

Stripe

Wooden beads

②Sew outer of bottom and ① with right sides together.

Quilting fabric

e
a
b
c
d
e

①Patchwork.   Stripe (Wrong side)

(Wrong side)
Cardboard
Batting
Stripe

b
Patchwork, Patchwork fablic on stripe.
(Right side)

(Right side)
a b c

Final joined pieces.

(Wrong side)

(Right side)

Blind stitch

3cm(1³⁄₁₆″) Border strip...Polka dots 1 piece
56cm×3cm(22″×(1³⁄₁₆″)   (seam 1cm(³⁄₈″))

56cm(22¹⁄₁₆″)

7cm(2³⁄₄″) Side section
Lining...Stripe 1 piece

Patchwork fabric   Seam allowance is 1cm(³⁄₈″)
(Refer to picture)

a.b.d.e.=3 pieces each c=2 pieces

7cm(2³⁄₄″)

a Polka dots	b Print Ⓑ	c Print on Red	d Check	e Print Ⓐ	a Polka dots	b Print Ⓑ	d Check	e Print Ⓐ

Repeat 2 times.
4cm(1⁹⁄₁₆″)

CONTINUED FROM PAGE 43

CUTTING DIAGRAM (ACTUAL SIZE)
☆Seam allowance is 0.8cm(⁵⁄₁₆″)
cut 1 piece for heart shape
Lining...Print 3 pieces

Opening for stuffing

Pattern B
(Refer to patchwork fabric for seam allowance)

Bag & Bag

Patchwork for fun!

This little patchwork patterns makes an exquisite bag.
You'll be proud of these handmade patchwork bags.

BAGS

Instructions on page 54

Simple, attractive, and handy bags great for many uses.

[ACTUAL SIZE]

"Winter dahlia" patchwork pattern .The 2 bags use different-sized patterns that are made the same easy way

Bag
Bag
page 52.53

Materials

	Little one	Big one
Blue gray quilting fabric	66cm×65cm(26″×25 ½″)	82cm×69cm(32 ¼″×27 ⅛″)
Blue gray print	30cm×20cm(11 ¹³⁄₁₆″×7 ⅞″)	30cm×25cm(11 ¹³⁄₁₆″×10″)
Pink print	25cm×20cm(10″×7 ⅞″)	35cm×20cm(13 ¾″×7 ⅞″)
Dark brown print	Little bit	
Old rose cotton	Little bit	
Quilt batting	40cm×37cm(15 ¾″×14 ½″)	40cm(15 ¾″)square
Quilt thread...Blue gray	Common	

Finished size . . . Refer to illustration

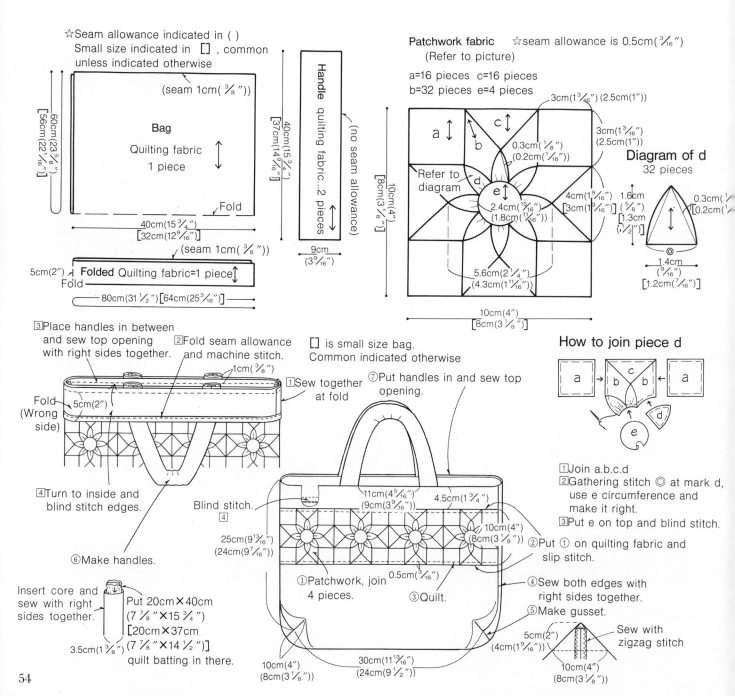

☆Seam allowance indicated in ( )
Small size indicated in [ ] , common unless indicated otherwise

(seam 1cm(⅜ ″))

Bag
Quilting fabric
1 piece

60cm(23 ⅝ ″) [56cm(22 ⅛ ″)]

Fold

40cm(15 ¾ ″) [32cm(12 ⁹⁄₁₆ ″)]

(seam 1cm(⅜ ″))

5cm(2″)
Fold
Folded Quilting fabric=1 piece
80cm(31 ½ ″) [64cm(25 ³⁄₁₆ ″)]

Handle quilting fabric..2 pieces
(no seam allowance)
40cm(15 ¾ ″) [37cm(14 ⁹⁄₁₆ ″)]
9cm (3 ⁹⁄₁₆ ″)

Patchwork fabric   ☆seam allowance is 0.5cm(³⁄₁₆ ″)
(Refer to picture)
a=16 pieces c=16 pieces
b=32 pieces e=4 pieces

3cm(1 ³⁄₁₆ ″) (2.5cm(1″))
3cm(1 ³⁄₁₆ ″) (2.5cm(1″))
0.3cm(⅛ ″) (0.2cm(¹⁄₁₆ ″))
Refer to diagram
4cm(1 ⁹⁄₁₆ ″) [3cm(1 ³⁄₁₆ ″)]
2.4cm(¹⁵⁄₁₆ ″) (1.8cm(¹¹⁄₁₆ ″))
5.6cm(2 ¼ ″) (4.3cm(1 ¹¹⁄₁₆ ″))
10cm(4″) [8cm(3 ⅛ ″)]
10cm(4″) [8cm(3 ⅛ ″)]

Diagram of d
32 pieces
0.3cm(⅛ ″) [0.2cm(¹⁄₁₆ ″)]
1.6cm (⅝ ″) [1.3cm (½ ″)]
1.4cm (⁹⁄₁₆ ″) [1.2cm(⁷⁄₁₆ ″)]

③Place handles in between and sew top opening with right sides together.
②Fold seam allowance and machine stitch.
1cm(⅜ ″)
[ ] is small size bag.
Common indicated otherwise

⑦Put handles in and sew top opening.

Fold (Wrong side)
5cm(2″)

④Turn to inside and blind stitch edges.

①Sew together at fold

Blind stitch.
④

⑥Make handles.

Insert core and sew with right sides together.
Put 20cm×40cm (7 ⅞ ″×15 ¾ ″) [20cm×37cm (7 ⅞ ″×14 ½ ″)] quilt batting in there.
3.5cm(1 ⅜ ″)

11cm(4 ⁵⁄₁₆ ″) (9cm(3 ⁹⁄₁₆ ″))
4.5cm(1 ¾ ″)
10cm(4″) (8cm(3 ⅛ ″))
25cm(9 ¹³⁄₁₆ ″) (24cm(9 ⁷⁄₁₆ ″))
①Patchwork, join 4 pieces.
0.5cm(³⁄₁₆ ″)
③Quilt.
10cm(4″) (8cm(3 ⅛ ″))
30cm(11 ¹³⁄₁₆ ″) (24cm(9 ½ ″))
5cm(2″) (4cm(1 ⁹⁄₁₆ ″))
10cm(4″) (8cm(3 ⅛ ″))

②Put ① on quilting fabric and slip stitch.
④Sew both edges with right sides together.
⑤Make gusset.
Sew with zigzag stitch

How to join piece d
a → b c b ← a
d
e

①Join a.b.c.d
②Gathering stitch ◎ at mark d, use e circumference and make it right.
③Put e on top and blind stitch.

54

EMBROIDERY DIAGRAM
(ACTUAL SIZE)
3 strands unless indicated
otherwise
Backstitch unless indicated
otherwise

House

‹DISH CASE›

1 strand

French knot
stitch

Straight stitch
1 strand

Straight stitch

Cherry

6 strands

My

Center

Favorite

Straight stitch
1 strand

Heart

French knot stitch

Straight stitch

French knot stitch

Cross stitch
2 strands

milk

Straight stitch
1 strand

‹DISH MAT›

Straight stitch
1 strand

Straight stitch
2 strands

Bear

Straight stitch
2 strands

2 strands

French knot
stitch
Straight stitch

Satin stitch

French knot stitch
2 strands

Bear

Straight stitch

Straight stitch
2 strands

Milk

House

2 strands

Straight stitch
2 strands

Cherry

Straight stitch
2 strands

Heart

Bag
BAG

Instructions on page 58

Different reflect your personal style.

The more you use them, the more you'll love them.!

Great for carrying almost anytime.!

Lined with red check quilting fabric.

[ACTUAL SIZE] Patchwork of "beggar block" and "four patch"

With only 4 tacks at the corners, and this easy to make patchwork becomes a bag.

Bag
BAG
page 56.57

Materials

Blue cotton 90cm×85cm(35 ½″×33 ½″)

Check quilting fabric 63cm(24 ¹³⁄₁₆″)square

Cotton for patchwork (Refer to picture)

30cm(11 ¹³⁄₁₆″)square each

Quilt batting 36cm×83cm(14 ³⁄₁₆″×32 ½″)

Button 2cm(¾″)diameter...1

Quilt thread...Offwhite

Finished size... Refer to illustration

☆Seam allowance is indicated in ( )

(seam 1cm(⅜″)) 10.5cm 7cm 11.3cm 7cm 10.5cm
(4⅛″) (2¾″) (4⁷⁄₁₆″) (2¾″) (4⅛″)

7cm (2¾″) Tuck A Tuck A Tuck 7cm (2¾″)

Outer...Blue
Lining...Quilting
1 each

B B

A Patchwork position A

B B

A A

Fold

60.3cm(23¾″)

60.3cm(23¾″)

6cm (2³⁄₈″)

Top...Blue 2 pieces ←→

1.6cm (⅝″)

28cm(11¹⁄₁₆″)

Quilt batting...Cut 12cm×30cm(4¾″×11¹³⁄₁₆″)2 pieces

Loop...Blue 1 piece

(1cm(⅜″))

(1cm(⅜″)) (0.8cm(⁵⁄₁₆″))

20cm(7⅞″)

6cm (2³⁄₈″)

(seam 1cm(⅜″))

Handle...Blue 2 pieces ←→

81cm(31⅞″)

Quilt batting...Cut 12cm×83cm(4¾″×32¹¹⁄₁₆″)2 pieces

Patchwork fabric ☆Seam allowance is 0.7cm(¼″)

A 10 blocks
a=40 pieces b.c= 20 pieces each

Quilt position

0.2cm (¹⁄₁₆″)

a

b

c c

b

6.7cm(2⅝″)

6.7cm(2⅝″)

B 8 blocks
a=16 pieces b=32 pieces c=8 pieces
c=8 pieces

b a

b

1.8cm C (¹¹⁄₁₆″) 1.8cm (¹¹⁄₁₆″)

6.7cm(2⅝″)

6.7cm(2⅝″)

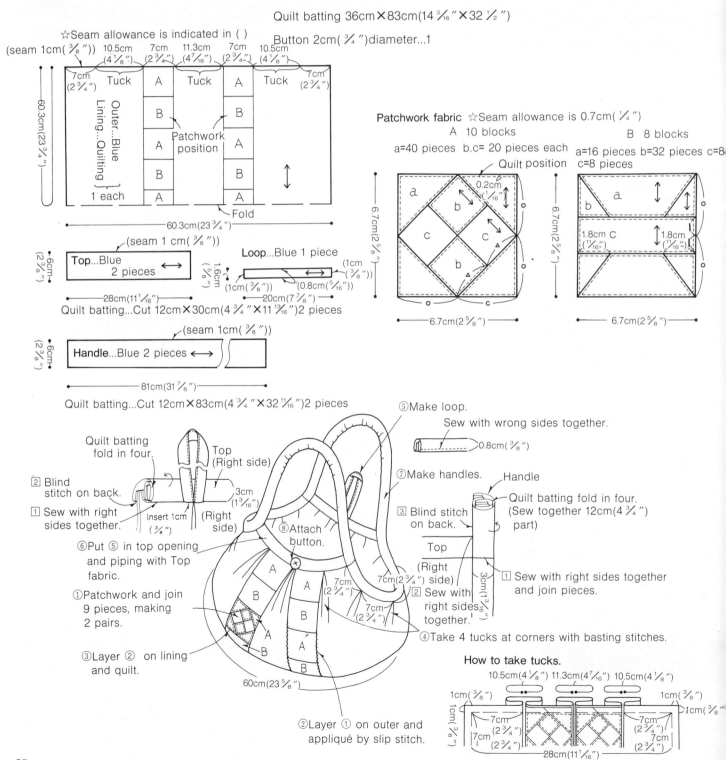

⑤Make loop.
Sew with wrong sides together.

0.8cm(⅜″)

⑦Make handles.

Handle

Quilt batting fold in four.
(Sew together 12cm(4¾″) part)

Top (Right side)

③ Blind stitch on back.

Quilt batting fold in four.

Top (Right side)

② Blind stitch on back.

① Sew with right sides together.

3cm (1³⁄₁₆″)

Insert 1cm (⅜″)

(Right side)

⑥Put ⑤ in top opening and piping with Top fabric.

①Patchwork and join 9 pieces, making 2 pairs.

③Layer ② on lining and quilt.

⑧Attach button.

A

B

A

B

A

B

7cm (2¾″)

7cm(2¾″)

7cm (2¾″)

Top (Right side) side)

② Sew with right sides together.

① Sew with right sides together and join pieces.

3cm(1³⁄₁₆″)

④Take 4 tucks at corners with basting stitches.

60cm(23⅝″)

②Layer ① on outer and appliqué by slip stitch.

How to take tucks.

10.5cm(4⅛″) 11.3cm(4⁷⁄₁₆″) 10.5cm(4⅛″)

1cm(⅜″)

1cm (⅜″)

1cm (⅜″)

7cm (2¾″)

7cm (2¾″)

7cm (2¾″)

7cm (2¾″)

1cm(⅜″)

28cm(11¹⁄₁₆″)

Kitchen
HANDY BAG
page 20.21

Materials

Olivegreen cotton...70cm×25cm
(27 ½ ″×10″)
Print on white cotton 90cm×35cm
(35 ½ ″×17 ¾ ″)
Quilt batting 60cm×30cm(23 ⅝ ″×11 ¹³⁄₁₆ ″)

Quilt thread...Offwhite

Button 1.5cm(⁹⁄₁₆ ″)diameter...2

Cardboard 18.4cm(7 ¼ ″)square

Glue

Finished size...Refer to illustration

☆Seam allowance indicated in ( )

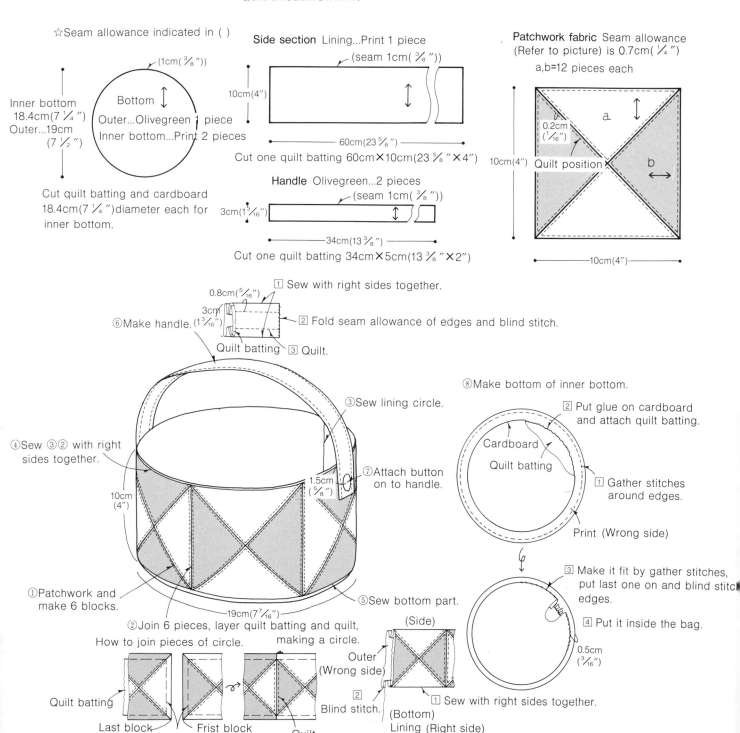

Inner bottom
18.4cm(7 ¼ ″)
Outer...19cm
(7 ½ ″)

(1cm(⅜ ″))

Bottom ↕
Outer...Olivegreen 1 piece
Inner bottom...Print 2 pieces

Cut quilt batting and cardboard
18.4cm(7 ¼ ″)diameter each for
inner bottom.

Side section Lining...Print 1 piece
(seam 1cm(⅜ ″))
10cm(4″)
60cm(23 ⅝ ″)
Cut one quilt batting 60cm×10cm(23 ⅝ ″×4″)

Handle Olivegreen...2 pieces
(seam 1cm(⅜ ″))
3cm(1 ³⁄₁₆ ″)
34cm(13 ⅜ ″)
Cut one quilt batting 34cm×5cm(13 ⅜ ″×2″)

Patchwork fabric Seam allowance
(Refer to picture) is 0.7cm(¼ ″)
a,b=12 pieces each
a
b
0.2cm
(¹⁄₁₆ ″)
Quilt position
10cm(4″)
10cm(4″)

① Sew with right sides together.
0.8cm(⁵⁄₁₆ ″)
3cm
(1 ³⁄₁₆ ″)
⑥Make handle.
Quilt batting
② Fold seam allowance of edges and blind stitch.
③ Quilt.

③Sew lining circle.
④Sew ③② with right sides together.
10cm(4″)
①Patchwork and make 6 blocks.
19cm(7 ⁷⁄₁₆ ″)
1.5cm(⁵⁄₈ ″)
⑦Attach button on to handle.
⑤Sew bottom part.

②Join 6 pieces, layer quilt batting and quilt, making a circle.
How to join pieces of circle.
Quilt batting
Last block   Frist block
Sew with right sides together.
Quilt

⑧Make bottom of inner bottom.
② Put glue on cardboard and attach quilt batting.
Cardboard
Quilt batting
① Gather stitches around edges.
Print (Wrong side)
③ Make it fit by gather stitches, put last one on and blind stitch edges.
④ Put it inside the bag.
0.5cm(³⁄₁₆ ″)

(Side)
Outer (Wrong side)
②Blind stitch.
① Sew with right sides together.
(Bottom)
Lining (Right side)

59

Bag
BAG

Instructions on page 62

Easy and useful patchwork bags.
Creative fabrics can make a great combination.
Same bag, but in different colors.

[ACTUAL SIZE] Square patchwork

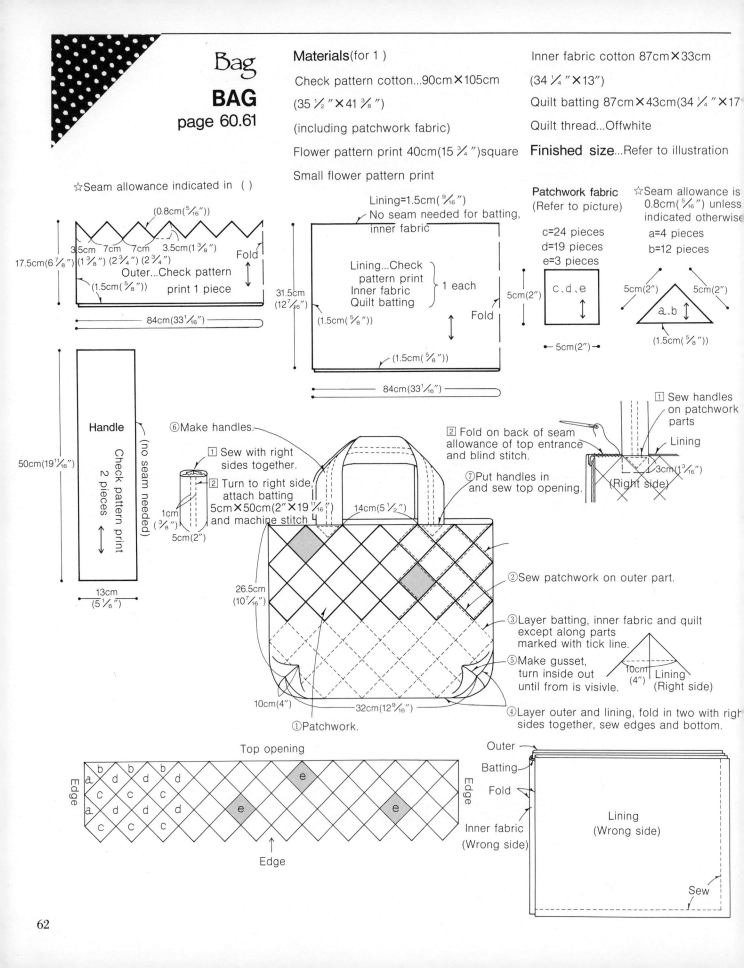

Bag
BAG
page 60.61

Materials(for 1)

Check pattern cotton...90cm×105cm

(35 ½″×41 ⅜″)

(including patchwork fabric)

Flower pattern print 40cm(15 ¾″)square

Small flower pattern print

Inner fabric cotton 87cm×33cm

(34 ¼″×13″)

Quilt batting 87cm×43cm(34 ¼″×17″)

Quilt thread...Offwhite

Finished size...Refer to illustration

Patchwork fabric
(Refer to picture)

c=24 pieces
d=19 pieces
e=3 pieces

a=4 pieces
b=12 pieces

☆Seam allowance indicated in ( )

(0.8cm(⁵⁄₁₆″))

3.5cm 7cm 7cm 3.5cm(1⅜″)
(1⅜″) (2¾″) (2¾″)

17.5cm(6⅞″)

Fold

Outer...Check pattern
print 1 piece

(1.5cm(⅝″))

84cm(33¹⁄₁₆″)

Lining=1.5cm(⁹⁄₁₆″)
No seam needed for batting,
inner fabric

Lining...Check
pattern print
Inner fabric
Quilt batting } 1 each

31.5cm
(12⁷⁄₁₆″)

(1.5cm(⅝″))

Fold

(1.5cm(⅝″))

84cm(33¹⁄₁₆″)

☆Seam allowance is
0.8cm(⁵⁄₁₆″) unless
indicated otherwise

5cm(2″)

c、d、e

←— 5cm(2″) —→

5cm(2″)   5cm(2″)

a、b

(1.5cm(⅝″))

Handle

Check pattern print
2 pieces

(no seam needed)

50cm(19¹¹⁄₁₆″)

13cm
(5⅛″)

⑥Make handles.

① Sew with right
sides together.

② Turn to right side,
attach batting
5cm×50cm(2″×19¹¹⁄₁₆″)
and machine stitch

1cm
(⅜″)

5cm(2″)

① Sew handles
on patchwork
parts

Lining

3cm(1³⁄₁₆″)

(Right side)

② Fold on back of seam
allowance of top entrance
and blind stitch.

⑦Put handles in
and sew top opening.

14cm(5½″)

②Sew patchwork on outer part.

③Layer batting, inner fabric and quilt
except along parts
marked with tick line.

⑤Make gusset,
turn inside out
until from is visivle.

10cm
(4″)

Lining
(Right side)

④Layer outer and lining, fold in two with right
sides together, sew edges and bottom.

26.5cm
(10⁷⁄₁₆″)

10cm(4″)

32cm(12⁹⁄₁₆″)

①Patchwork.

Top opening

b b b
a d d d
c c c c
a d d d e
c c c c

e

e

Edge

Edge

Edge

Outer
Batting
Fold
Inner fabric
(Wrong side)

Lining
(Wrong side)

Sew

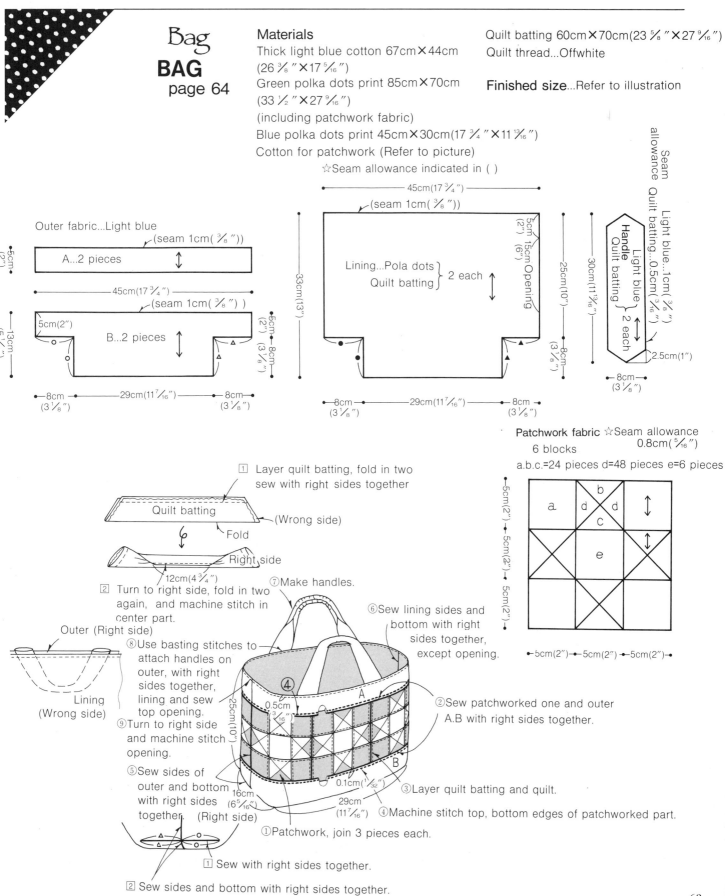

Bag
BAG
page 64

Materials

Thick light blue cotton 67cm×44cm
(26 3/8″×17 5/16″)
Green polka dots print 85cm×70cm
(33 1/2″×27 9/16″)
(including patchwork fabric)
Blue polka dots print 45cm×30cm(17 3/4″×11 13/16″)
Cotton for patchwork (Refer to picture)
☆Seam allowance indicated in ( )

Quilt batting 60cm×70cm(23 5/8″×27 9/16″)
Quilt thread...Offwhite

Finished size...Refer to illustration

Outer fabric...Light blue
(seam 1cm(3/8″))
A...2 pieces

5cm
(2″)

45cm(17 3/4″)
(seam 1cm(3/8″))
B...2 pieces
13cm
(5 1/8″)
5cm(2″)
5cm(2″)
8cm
(3 1/8″)
8cm
(3 1/8″)
29cm(11 7/16″)
8cm
(3 1/8″)

Seam allowance Quilt batting...
45cm(17 3/4″)
(seam 1cm(3/8″))
Lining...Pola dots } 2 each
Quilt batting
33cm(13″)
5cm
(2″)
15cm Opening
(6″)
25cm(10″)
8cm
(3 1/8″)
8cm
(3 1/8″)
29cm(11 7/16″)
8cm
(3 1/8″)

Seam allowance
Quilt batting
Light blue...1cm(3/8″)
Quilt batting...0.5cm(3/16″)
Handle
Light blue
Quilt batting } 2 each
30cm(11 13/16″)
2.5cm(1″)
8cm
(3 1/8″)

① Layer quilt batting, fold in two
sew with right sides together

Quilt batting
(Wrong side)
Fold
Right side
12cm(4 3/4″)

② Turn to right side, fold in two
again, and machine stitch in
center part.

Outer (Right side)
Lining
(Wrong side)

⑧ Use basting stitches to
attach handles on
outer, with right
sides together,
lining and sew
top opening.

⑨ Turn to right side
and machine stitch
opening.

⑤ Sew sides of
outer and bottom
with right sides
together. (Right side)

⑦ Make handles.

⑥ Sew lining sides and
bottom with right
sides together,
except opening.

④
0.5cm
(3/16″)
A
25cm(10″)
16cm
(6 5/16″)
B
0.1cm(1/32″)

② Sew patchworked one and outer
A.B with right sides together.

③ Layer quilt batting and quilt.

④ Machine stitch top, bottom edges of patchworked part.

① Patchwork, join 3 pieces each.

① Sew with right sides together.

② Sew sides and bottom with right sides together.

Patchwork fabric ☆Seam allowance
6 blocks 0.8cm(5/16″)
a.b.c.=24 pieces d=48 pieces e=6 pieces

5cm(2″)
5cm(2″)
5cm(2″)
a
b
d d
c
e

5cm(2″) 5cm(2″) 5cm(2″)

29cm
(11 7/16″)

Bag
Bag

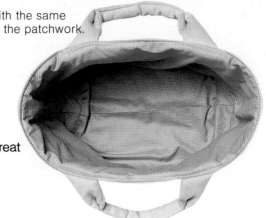

This bag is lined with the same polka dots used in the patchwork.

Instructions on page 63

An easy attractive handmade bag great for everything.
Doing patchwork is now my hobby.

"OHIO STAR" patchwork.